The Resurrection of Jesus

Jesus Seminar Guides

Bernard Brandon Scott, series editor

Published volumes

Volume 1: Jesus Reconsidered: Scholarship in the Public Eye

Volume 2: Listening to the Parables of Jesus

Volume 3: Finding the Historical Jesus: Rules of Evidence

Volume 4: The Resurrection of Jesus: A Sourcebook

The Resurrection of Jesus

A Sourcebook

Bernard Brandon Scott, editor

POLEBRIDGE PRESS
Santa Rosa, California

Copyright © 2008 by Polebridge Press

Cover and interior design by Robaire Ream

Library of Congress Cataloging-in-Publication Data
The Resurrection of Jesus : a sourcebook / Bernard Brandon Scott, editor.
    p. cm. -- (Jesus seminar guides ; v. 4)
Includes bibliographical references.
ISBN 978-1-59815-013-1 (alk. paper)
1. Jesus Christ--Resurrection--History of doctrines--Early church, ca. 30-600. 2. Jesus Christ--Historicity. 3. Jesus Seminar. I. Scott, Bernard Brandon, 1941-
BT482.R45 2008
232.9'7--dc22
                                                        2008049380

Table of Contents

Series Preface

Westar Institute, the home of the Jesus Seminar, is an advocate for literacy in religion and the Bible. A member-supported, non-profit research and educational institute, its mission is to foster collaborative research in religious studies and to communicate the results of the scholarship of religion to a broad, non-specialist public. Through publications, educational programs, and research projects like the Jesus Seminar, Westar brings Fellows of the Institute—scholars with advanced degrees in biblical studies, religion, or related fields—into conversation with non-specialists from all walks of life.

Westar's series, *Jesus Seminar Guides*, is designed to gather the best writings of Westar Fellows from the pages of its membership magazine, *The Fourth R*, its academic journal, *Forum*, and occasionally from previously unpublished material. Arranged topically, the *Guides* summarize the important questions and debates that have driven the work of the Jesus Seminar over the last twenty years. They are intended for use in classrooms, discussion groups inside and outside churches, and for the general reader.

Contributors

Arthur J. Dewey (Ph.D. Harvard University) is Professor of Theology, Xavier University and a commentator on the Saturday *Morning Edition* on public radio station WVXU (91.7), Cincinnati, OH. He also writes a regular editorial for *The Fourth R*.

Robert W. Funk (Ph.D. Vanderbilt University) was the founder of the Jesus Seminar and the Westar Institute. A Guggenheim Fellow and Senior Fulbright Scholar, he served as Annual Professor of the American School of Oriental Research in Jerusalem and as chair of the Graduate Department of Religion at Vanderbilt University. A recognized pioneer in modern biblical scholarship, Funk led the Society of Biblical Literature as its Executive Secretary from 1968–1973. His many books include *The Five Gospels* (1993) and *The Acts of Jesus* (1996) (both with the Jesus Seminar) and *Honest to Jesus* (1996), *A Credible Jesus* (2002), and *Funk on Parables* (2006).

Roy W. Hoover (Ph.D. Harvard University) is Weyerhaeuser Professor of Biblical Literature and Professor of Religion Emeritus, Whitman College. A Fellow of the Jesus Seminar since 1986, he wrote a number of the papers that served as the basis for the Seminar's deliberations and has been a frequent participant in the Jesus Seminar on the Road Program. Hoover is co-author with Robert Funk of *The Five Gospels* (1993), and editor of *Profiles of Jesus* (2002). His published articles have appeared in *Harvard Theological Review, The Fourth R,* and *Bible Review*.

Robert M. Price (Ph.D. Drew University) is Professor of Theology and Scriptural Studies at Johnnie Coleman Theological Seminary. The founding editor of *The Journal of*

Higher Criticism, he is the author of *The Widow Traditions in Luke-Acts* (1997), *Deconstructing Jesus* (1999), and *The Incredible Shrinking Son of Man* (2003).

Bernard Brandon Scott (Ph.D. Vanderbilt University) is the Darbeth Distinguished Professor of New Testament at the Phillips Theological Seminary, Tulsa, Oklahoma. He is the author of several books, including *Hear Then the Parable* (1989), *Re-Imagine the World* (2002) and *Hollywood Dreams and Biblical Stories* (1994). *The Parables of Jesus: Red Letter Edition* (co-edited with Robert Funk and James R. Butts, 1988), the first report of the Jesus Seminar, as well as *Reading New Testament Greek* (co-authored with a group of students, 1993), and was the editor of Robert Funk, *Funk on Parables* (2006).

Thomas Sheehan (Ph.D. Fordham University) is Professor, Department of Religious Studies, Stanford University and specializes in contemporary European philosophy and its relation to religious questions, with particular interests in Heidegger and Roman Catholicism. His books include: *Becoming Heidegger* (2007), *Edmund Husserl: Psychological and Transcendental Phenomenology and the Encounter with Heidegger* (1997), *Karl Rahner: The Philosophical Foundations* (1987), *The First Coming: How the Kingdom of God Became Christianity* (1986), and *Heidegger, the Man and the Thinker* (1981).

Introduction

Bernard Brandon Scott

What should be your first step if you want to understand what resurrection meant in early Christianity? I would suggest that the first step is to excise from your imagination all of the Christian art you have seen about the resurrection. Those images of Thomas thrusting his hand into the side of Jesus, or the two disciples walking along the road to Emmaus with Jesus, or Mary being told not to cling to Jesus. Then forget all the sermons you have heard at Easter.

If you want to understand what resurrection meant and how it emerged in early Christianity, the first step is to arrange the relevant texts in chronological order so that you can see the pattern that develops. Since popular piety ignores this essential step, the dramatic scenes found in the gospels of Luke and John, which are among the latest texts in the New Testament, have come to dominate people's thinking, especially because the Easter lectionary readings and famous artworks come predominantly from these two gospels. To come to terms with the early Christian concept of resurrection, we must struggle against the distortions thus created. In short, we must let early Christian experience and faith emerge from the text, not impose later positions or views on it.

This *Jesus Seminar Guide* is a sourcebook on resurrection. It provides you with the texts and discussions of those texts so that you can come to an informed opinion concerning the emergence of the Christian view of resurrection in the first two centuries.

1

Robert W. Funk in "The Resurrection of Jesus: Reports and Stories" includes all the relevant texts in approximate chronological order. For each text he provides a brief description. Having all the texts together in one place is of great benefit since it enables you to see how the texts are similar and different, and the chronological arrangement affords the reader a different perspective on the tradition. Since we are accustomed to dealing with the texts all jumbled together, this chronological arrangement imposes a salutary discipline on our reading.

The New Testament accounts of resurrection employ three types or genres of literature: lists, reports, and stories. At the earliest level are simple lists of those who experienced the resurrected Jesus. Next come reports of those to whom Jesus appeared, and finally come the still later stories of appearances of the resurrected Jesus. These types of accounts are not only formally different, but they appear in different chronological levels. The distinctions that Funk makes are crucial in enabling us to form an impression of how the resurrection tradition developed in early Christianity.

Funk takes you through all the early texts dealing with the resurrection of Jesus. If you are discussing this in a group, you might want to take more than one session to cover all these texts, for the essay covers a great deal of material and its chronological organization is counter-intuitive to the traditional way of viewing the resurrection. I have provided a detailed list of Discussion Questions at the back of this book in an effort to help guide you through the issues involved in understanding these various texts. Above all, do not think to yourself, "I already know this material" and skip this collection of texts. It is the foundation for everything that follows.

At the Spring 1995 meeting of the Jesus Seminar, the resurrection of Jesus was discussed and voted on. Dealing with this issue was very different from dealing with individual sayings attributed to Jesus, for the issues are complex and highly debatable. First comes a summary of the discussions and votes. Both of these give you a good idea of the range of issues involved and the variety of opinions on these issues. Reading the results of the votes can at first be surprising and even shocking. But if you have worked through the texts about the resurrection from the New Testament

in Funk's preceding article, you will begin to see why this group
of scholars came to these conclusions.

Resurrection is not a uniquely Christian phenomenon.
Resurrection from the dead is well attested in Judaism. Alan Segal
in his monumental study, *Life after Death: A History of Afterlife in
Western Religion* (2004) traces the development of this notion
through its various twists and turns. Segal's view is encyclopedic
and Roy Hoover in chapter 5 of this volume provides a short
view of this material. Robert M. Price in "Brand X Easters"
focuses on parallel accounts from the Greco-Roman world. These
accounts enable us to see the great variety of models available to
early Christians as they attempted to understand and give literary expression to their experiences. Some may find Price's style
disturbingly blunt; he sets forth his point of view without minc-
ing words. But he is presenting these parallels for consideration so
that you can decide how to evaluate the evidence. Take him up
on his offer.

Where Price concentrates on the Greek parallels to the resurrection stories, Arthur Dewey moves in a very different direction.
He is probing the origin of the resurrection tradition and sees it
as deeply embedded in the martyr tradition of Judaism. That tradition, beginning with the Maccabees, had asked whether it was
conceivable that God's righteous ones should utterly lose their
lives at the hands of their enemies. God's ultimate vindication of
the righteous through resurrection was the solution.

Considerable controversy has swirled around the Gospel of
Peter. A fragmentary Greek manuscript of this gospel discovered
in the late nineteenth century can be dated to eighth or ninth
century, though because the text is fragmentary dating the gospel
is difficult. Still, it was known and quoted in the last half of the
second century. (For English translation, introduction and notes
see Miller, *The Complete Gospels*, 399–410.)

In the opinion of some, this gospel is late and is dependent on
the canonical gospels (see, e.g., Brown 1987, 1993). But this solution is problematical, for several aspects of the Gospel of Peter
cannot be easily derived from the canonical gospels. These issues
have led some scholars to argue that elements of the gospel of
Peter are independent of and/or predate the canonical gospels
(Koester 1983, Crossan 1988, Dewey 1990). If their conclusions

are valid, these early elements predate the gospel of Mark, but are subsequent to Paul's account in 1 Corinthians 15.

Arthur Dewey has been a leader in the analysis of the Gospel of Peter. His essay takes you through this gospel step by step, raising and analyzing all the relevant issues. This essay, which originally appeared in *Forum*, the scholarly journal of the Jesus Seminar, has been rewritten to make it more accessible to the readers of *Jesus Seminar Guides*. Nonetheless, it deals with all the texts in the Gospel of Peter that are relevant to the topic of resurrection. By following Dewey's careful analysis you can obtain a good grasp of the issues, and you will see that the Gospel of Peter is a valuable source in helping you understand the development of resurrection.

Dewey's essay, the most difficult one in this volume, will require concentration and effort. In formulating the Discussion Questions I have attempted to lead you through the argument. The essay begins with all of the text from the Gospel of Peter that deals with the death and exaltation of Jesus. Dewey argues that behind the text we now have lies an earlier version, one that he reconstructs and that he considers a source for the canonical Gospels. If that is true, it is both the earliest resurrection account and the only one that depicts the actual event. Pay close attention to the argument, because it is a good example of how scholars go about reconstructing such hypothetical texts. Whether you agree with the result or not, you will be thinking through a major issue: how the early followers of Jesus came to terms in language with what they experienced as the events surrounding the death of Jesus and God's response to that death.

For Dewey the earliest resurrection text is:

> "My power, <my> power, you have abandoned me." When he said this, he was taken up. (Gospel of Peter 5.5)

"He was taken up" is a reference not to Jesus' death but to his exaltation. Exaltation is an important part of the pattern of the suffering and vindication of the righteous one who suffers martyrdom. A major point in Dewey's essay, though one he does not stress, is the connection between the death of Jesus (suffering at the hand of the unrighteous) and his vindication (exaltation). Without the death there is no need for the exaltation. Without the type of death Jesus dies, there is no need for God's vindica-tion. What Dewey makes clear is that resurrection is always an answer to the problem of the death of Jesus. Except in the context of that death and the type of death it was, resurrection makes no sense.

Roy Hoover's "Wasn't Jesus' Resurrection an Historical Event?" is his part of debate with evangelical scholar Craig Evans. Hoover argues that the faith in the resurrection of Jesus was supported by the appearances of the resurrected Jesus. The appearances did not generate faith in the resurrection. Faith was prior.

Resurrection, he notes, is a private event. Had CNN existed in the ancient world, it could have broadcast the crucifixion, but not the resurrection. Jesus appears nowhere in public. Because the gospels so disagree in their retelling of the resurrection, it means that there is no common tradition behind them.

Thomas Sheehan, a philosopher of religion, presents two essays that will help you put the pieces together. The first, "The Resurrection, An Obstacle to Faith?", takes aim at the fundamentalist assertion that Jesus' resurrection was both historical and physical. He charges literalists with making a fantastical assumption, and then demonstrates that the early accounts do not support these assumptions.

Sheehan reinforces one of Dewey's major points: he puts "resurrection" in quotation marks because he wants to indicate that the word itself is a problem. The Easter story does not begin with a resurrection: as Dewey argues and Sheehan now reinforces, the earliest notion is not "resurrection" but "exaltation." In Sheehan's model "resurrection" occurs only in the second stage of the developing tradition; and as he points out, the primary meaning of the Greek word used here is "to wake up" or "to get up." Sheehan's use of the term Easter victory to represent the original experience/event also reinforces Dewey's point that both "exaltation" and "resurrection" are responses to the death of Jesus.

Sheehan's second essay, "How Did Easter Originally Happen? A Hypothesis," moves in a very different direction. Sheehan constructs an original hypothesis to explain how early Christians came to believe in the resurrection. A hypothesis, of course, is a way of explaining the gaps in the evidence and of filling in those gaps so as to make sense of the evidence we do have. And every hypothesis must be tested against the evidence.

For Sheehan the Easter accounts are myths, but he accepts the reality of some kind of transformative experience on the part of those first believers. He argues that something happened that "convinced them that Jesus continued to exercise power after his death." To put it another way, they were convinced that Rome had not triumphed over Jesus in the crucifixion, but that God had vindicated him. Everything else, Sheehan concludes, is elaboration.

Chapter One

The Resurrection of Jesus

Reports and Stories

Robert W. Funk

S tatements about Jesus' resurrection are preserved for us in three forms. The first consists of a list of those to whom Jesus appeared. In the second, an appearance to an individual or group is reported but not depicted. In the third, an appearance of the risen Jesus is described. We thus have lists, reports, and stories.

The resurrection of Jesus from the dead is not itself narrated in the New Testament gospels as a specific event; rather, it is announced as something that took place previously. By way of exception, however, the emergence of Jesus (or some cosmic figure) from the tomb is depicted in the Gospel of Peter 9–10. In the Gospel of the Hebrews 9, following his resurrection, Jesus is described as handing his shroud to a slave of the high priest and then appearing first to James, his brother.

The resurrection of Jesus is most commonly affirmed in stories of his appearances to his disciples. In some cases, the appearances are not depicted but merely asserted. Combining all the lists,

The Fourth R 7,4 (July/August 1994), pp. 3–16.

reports, and stories, we have the following catalogue of reported appearances:

To one or more women (Matt, Luke, John 20)
To Simon Peter/Cephas (Paul, Luke)
To the twelve or eleven (Paul, Matt, Luke)
To more than 500 believers at the same time (Paul)
To James (Paul, GHeb)
To all the apostles (Paul, Luke)
To Paul (Paul, Luke)
To two on the road to Emmaus (Luke)
To Thomas (John 20)
To Peter and six on the Sea of Galilee (John 21)
To Peter, James, and John (Mark 9 and parallels)
To Stephen (Acts)
To John on the island of Patmos (Revelation)

This list is derived primarily from 1 Corinthians 15:3–8, but is supplemented by Luke 24, John 20–21, the transfiguration story, Acts 7, and Revelation. We cannot be sure of the number of appearances because we cannot determine for sure which stories are duplicates and which represent distinct appearances.

Primary Texts and Stories

The lists, stories, and reports on which this list is based include the following:

1. 1 Corinthians 15:3–8
2. 1 Corinthians 15:40, 42, 44, 47–48, 50
3. Mark 16:1–8
4. Matthew 28:1–20
5. Luke 24:1–53
6. Acts 1:1–11
7. John 20:1–31
8. John 21:1–23
9. Gospel of Peter 9–14
10. Gospel of the Hebrews 9
11. Pseudo-Mark 16:9–20
12. Mark 9:2–8; Matthew 17:1–8; Luke 9:28–36

13. Luke 5:1–11
14. Acts 9:3–19; 22:1–16; 26:9–18
15. Acts 7:55–56
16. Revelation 1:13–16

In assessing the nature of these reports we should have all the primary texts before us. To that end, I have collected here the texts and to each I have added a brief commentary indicating some of the salient features of that report.

Helpful Definitions

It may be helpful at the outset to point out three varieties of appearances or what are often called epiphanies. First of all, there are angelophanies—the report of the appearance of a heavenly messenger. Second, there are christophanies—reports of the risen Jesus as a heavenly figure exhibiting the same characteristics as the heavenly messengers. And, finally, there are also theophanies—literally, "appearances of God," which are always auditory rather than visual since, in the Hebrew tradition, God cannot be depicted: the recipients hear a voice and see only a bright light. To these definitions we should perhaps add the term protophany, which scholars employ to denote the first or initiating appearance. In early Christian tradition the protophany of Jesus is to Mary, or Peter, or James.

The Reports: An Overview

The earliest reference we have is a list of appearances recorded in Paul's first letter to the Corinthians, written in the mid-50s. In the same letter, Paul also provides a rather lengthy sketch of how he conceives of the resurrection, both that of Jesus and that of all believers. The first account of the empty tomb and the promise of appearances in Galilee is found in the Gospel of Mark, composed in the decade of the 70s. Matthew and Luke of course make use of Mark, although Luke draws on additional stories for his string of appearances. The Gospel of John is an anomaly, as usual: the reports in chapters 20 and 21 clearly stem from different lines of tradition. For that reason many scholars think that the Fourth Gospel originally ended with chapter 20.

Luke also provides additional reports in the book of Acts, notably three accounts of Jesus' appearance to Paul on the road to Damascus. Some scholars think that the Pentecost story in Acts may originally have been the appearance to 500 believers all at once mentioned by Paul. Others list the vision of Stephen in Acts 7 as an account of another apparition.

The Gospel of Mark originally ended with 16:8—with the story of the empty tomb but without the narration of an appearance of the risen Jesus. But early storytellers or scribes provided additional endings for Mark that reported appearances to remedy what was thought to be a deficiency.

Some scholars also regard the account of Peter's call in Luke 5:1–11 to be a misplaced resurrection story. Its counterpart is found in John 21. Accordingly, I have included the Lukan call story among the texts to be considered.

In addition, the transfiguration of Jesus in the presence of Peter, James, and John in Mark 9 and parallels is often thought to be another misplaced appearance story. We must therefore include these texts among the stories to be evaluated.

The Gospel of Peter has a rather extended account of the actual resurrection of Jesus in chapters 6–14. This narrative will undoubtedly play a significant role in the deliberations of the Seminar.

The Gospel of the Hebrews 9 also has a report of Jesus handing the linen cloth that was used to cover him to the high priest's slave. That report is quoted by Jerome and is included among the primary texts.

Finally, we should examine reports of appearances to another John on the island of Patmos towards the end of the century.

1   1 Corinthians 15:3–8

An Early List of Appearances

³Among the very first things I passed on to you was what I myself also received as tradition: Christ died for our sins according to the scriptures, ⁴and was buried, and rose on the third day according to the scriptures. ⁵He then appeared to Cephas and later to the twelve. ⁶Next he appeared to a crowd of more than 500 believers at the same time, most of whom are still alive, although some have died. ⁷Subsequently he appeared to James and then to all the apostles. ⁸Last of all, like the freak of nature I am, he appeared to me as well.

Gospel stories of Jesus' appearance after his death to individuals and groups are not the first evidence we have of such apparitions. The earliest list of such appearances is found in Paul's first letter to the Corinthians, written in the mid-50s.

At this stage, there are only reports of appearances; there are no stories describing them. Narratives of appearances were to come perhaps thirty years later with the creation of the Gospel of Matthew. The Gospel of Mark, which precedes Matthew, tells of the visit of the women to an empty tomb and the testimony of an angelic figure, but Mark does not depict an appearance of the risen Jesus.

Several things about Paul's list are worthy of note.

First, the list is something Paul himself did not apparently create; he had received it, or part of it, as lore passed on to him after his own conversion. We do not know how old it is. We can only say that Paul knew of it at the time he established the congregation in Corinth, about 50 CE, since he reminds the Corinthians that he had passed some or all of that information on to them earlier.

Second, we cannot tell how much of the list Paul learned from his predecessors and how much is his own addition or additions. It is possible that the old lore ended with references to Jesus' death and resurrection (vv. 3–4); it may have included the reference to Cephas and the twelve (v. 5). Obviously the original list did not include Paul himself (v. 8).

The third thing to notice is that Paul provides no information about where these appearances occurred or when they occurred. Moreover, he does not tell us anything about their nature, other than what he says about resurrection generally in his discussion of the subject in the rest of chapter fifteen.

Finally, it is important to observe that the resurrection appearances are associated in Paul's mind with the formation of the Christian proclamation, for which we use the Greek term *kerygma*: Christ died for our sins in accordance with the scripture and arose on the third day also in accordance with scripture (1 Cor 15:3–4). That two-pronged statement, death/resurrection, became the rallying formulation of the Christian movement under Paul's tutelage. Succinctly put, Paul saw Jesus' death as an event with redemptive significance, and his resurrection was not only vindication for Jesus, but, more importantly, the promise of vindication for all believers at the end of history. In other words, as Dominic Crossan puts it, we owe Christian preoccupation with the resurrection of Jesus to Paul's way of linking it to our own future fate.

It is habitual with New Testament scholars to analyze the accounts of Jesus' resurrection without reference to the resurrection of other human beings, but it is a serious error not to consider the link between the two as of seminal importance.

2   1 Corinthians 15:40, 42, 44, 47–48, 50

The Resurrected Body

⁴⁰There are heavenly bodies and there are earthly bodies. But the external appearance of the celestial differs from that of the earthly. . . .

⁴²It is the same with the resurrection of the dead. It is planted as something subject to decay, but raised as something imperishable. . . .

⁴⁴It is planted as a physical body but raised as a spiritual body. . . .

⁴⁷The first man was made of dust; the second is made of heavenly material. ⁴⁸All who are made of dust are like the man of dust; those who are made of heavenly material are like the heavenly man. . . .

⁵⁰Let me tell you this, my friends: flesh and blood have no place in God's domain. Similarly, the perishable has no place with the imperishable.

Paul's lengthy exposition of the nature of the resurrected body extends from 15:37 to 15:57. I have included here only a few of the key contrasts. It is clear that for Paul the resurrected body will not be a resuscitated corpse.

3   Mark 16:1–8

Women at the Tomb

And when the sabbath day was over, Mary of Magdala and Mary the mother of James and Salome bought spices so they could go and embalm him. [2]And very early on Sunday they got to the tomb just as the sun was coming up. [3]And they had been asking themselves, "Who will help us roll the stone away from the opening of the tomb?" [4]Then they look up and discover that the stone has been rolled away! (For in fact the stone was very large.)

[5]And when they went into the tomb, they saw a young man sitting on the right, wearing a white robe, and they grew apprehensive.

[6]He says to them, "Don't be alarmed! You are looking for Jesus the Nazarene who was crucified. He was raised, he is not here! Look at the spot where they put him! [7]But go and tell his disciples, including 'Rock,' He is going ahead of you to Galilee! There you will see him, just as he told you."

[8]And once they got outside, they ran away from the tomb, because great fear and excitement got the better of them. And they didn't breathe a word of it to anyone: talk about terrified. . . .

The earliest narrative allusion to Jesus' resurrection is this story of the empty tomb preserved by Mark. What is narrated here is usually interpreted as an angelophany: the appearance of a creature from what the ancients thought of as the world above, the heavens. White garments are the uniform of a heavenly messenger or angel (derived ultimately from divine glory or radiance, Daniel 7:9, Mark 9:3). However, it is possible that this figure in Mark is to be understood merely as a young man, perhaps the one who had accompanied Jesus during his final hours (Mark 14:51–52).

The scene is set in Jerusalem. It is Sunday morning, scarcely forty-eight hours after the death of Jesus. The women come to the tomb to embalm the body. The angel appears and tells them that Jesus is risen and that he will appear to his disciples in Galilee. But, Mark instructs his readers, the women didn't report this to anyone. And Mark ends at this tantalizing point.

4 Matthew 28:1–20

A Women at the Tomb, vv. 1–8

After the sabbath day, at first light on Sunday, Mary of Magdala and the other Mary came to inspect the tomb. [2]And just then there was a strong earthquake. You see, a messenger of the Lord had come down from the sky, arrived <at the tomb>, rolled away the stone, and was sitting on it. [3]The messenger gave off a dazzling light and wore clothes as white as snow. [4]Now those who kept watch were paralyzed with fear and looked like corpses themselves.

[5]In response the messenger said to the women, "Don't be frightened! I know you are looking for Jesus who was crucified. [6]He is not here! You see, he was raised, just as he said. Come, look at the spot where he was lying. [7]And run, tell his disciples that he has been raised from the dead. Don't forget, he is going ahead of you to Galilee. There you will see him. Now I have told you so."

[8]And they hurried away from the tomb, full of apprehension and an overpowering joy, and ran to tell his disciples.

The Gospel of Mark was written sometime in the 70s of the first century. Matthew was composed perhaps a decade later, using Mark as the narrative framework. In addition to inserting material from the Sayings Gospel Q into Mark's outline, Matthew has edited Mark's narrative in a variety of ways, including both expansion and contraction.

Matthew's first scene in the resurrection narratives is based on the corresponding story in Mark. Matthew has not only added legendary material (vv. 2–4) to Mark's account, but has also altered it in important details.

Matthew has dramatized the angelophany with an earthquake, to make sure his readers understand the ground-shaking nature of that event. The angel is not sitting in the tomb as in Mark, but is sitting on the stone used to block the entrance. Matthew describes the angel and provides guards at the tomb who are also to be witnesses.

The women are not silent as in Mark, but run and report to the disciples.

B Appearance to the Women, vv. 9–10

[9]And then Jesus met them saying, "Hello!"
They came up and took hold of his feet and paid him homage.
[10]Then Jesus says to them, "Don't be afraid. Go tell my companions so they can leave for Galilee, where they will see me."

Verses 9 and 10 are evidently a Matthean addition. There is no basis for this story in Mark, and it clearly contradicts the tradition that the first appearance was to Peter, as reported by Paul, and that it took place in Galilee, as predicted by the young man in white garments in Mark and narrated in John 21. Moreover, in Matthew Jesus actually appears to the women as they depart the scene and tells them what the angel had told them in Mark's account.

This is perhaps the first time an angelophany has been turned into a christophany: the appearance of an angel becomes an appearance of Jesus now as the vindicated and glorified Christ.

C Bribing the Soldiers, vv. 11–15

[11]While they were on their way, some of the guards returned to the city and reported to the ranking priests everything that had happened. [12]They met with the elders and hatched a plan: they bribed the soldiers with an adequate amount of money [13]and ordered them: "Tell everybody that his disciples came at night and stole his body while we were asleep. [14]If the governor should hear about this, we will deal with him; you need have no worries." [15]They took the money and did as they had been instructed. And this story has been passed around among the Jews until this very day.

Matthew has added a further legendary element to the growing tradition with this tale of the bribed soldiers. According to Matthew, there was a rumor that Jesus' disciples had stolen his body. Matthew counters that rumor with this story about how the guards, who were actually witnesses to the angelophany, were in fact bribed to lie about their experience.

D Appearance to the Eleven in Galilee, vv. 16–20

[16]The eleven disciples went to the mountain in Galilee where Jesus had told them to go. [17]And when they saw him, they paid him homage; but some were dubious.

[18]And Jesus approached them and spoke these words: "All authority has been given to me in heaven and on earth. [19]You are to go and make followers of all peoples. You are to baptize them in the name of the Father and the son and the holy spirit. [20]Teach them to observe everything I commanded. I'll be with you day in and day out, as you'll see, so long as this world continues its course."

Matthew finally gets to the Galilean appearance that Mark promised but did not narrate: Jesus appears to the eleven on a mountain in Galilee, perhaps the same mountain where he delivered the great sermon. By speaking authoritatively from the sacred mountain, Jesus is made the successor to Moses, who received the Ten Commandments on a mountain.

As the new Moses, Jesus commissions his disciples to evangelize the world—a commission formulated, however, by Matthew or his community.

The appearance to Cephas or Peter is not narrated by either Mark or Matthew, indeed not by any source that has survived. We cannot tell whether the second appearance in Paul's list—to the twelve—is the same as Matthew's appearance to the eleven. The discrepancy between the numbers eleven and twelve is not significant in view of the desertion of Judas.

5 Luke 24:1–53

A Women at the Tomb, vv. 1–8

On Sunday, at daybreak, they made their way to the tomb, bringing the spices they had prepared. [2]They found the stone rolled away from the tomb, [3]but when they went inside they did not find the body of the Lord Jesus.

[4]And so, while they were still uncertain about what to do, two figures in dazzling clothing suddenly appeared and stood beside them. [5]Out of sheer fright they prostrated themselves on the ground; the men said to them, "Why are you looking for the living among the dead? [6]He is not here—he was raised. Remember what he told you while he was still in Galilee: [7]'The son of Adam is destined to be turned over to heathen, to be crucified, and on the third day to rise.'" [8]Then they recalled what he had said.

Luke has adopted and modified Mark's story. A single figure at the tomb has become two. Luke repeats his theme: Jesus had told them that he would be crucified and raised on the third day.

B The Women Report to the Eleven, vv. 9–11

[9]And returning from the tomb, they related everything to the eleven and to everybody else. [10]The group included Mary of Magdala and Joanna and Mary the mother of James, and the rest of the women companions. They related their story to the apostles; [11]but their story seemed nonsense to them, so they refused to believe the women.

Like Matthew but in contradiction to Mark, Luke has the women report to the eleven, who refuse to believe.

C Peter at the Tomb, v. 12

[12]But Peter got up and ran to the tomb. He peeped in and saw only the linen wrappings, and returned home, marveling at what had happened.

Verse 12 may not be a part of the original text of Luke: it does not appear in all ancient manuscripts. And it appears to contradict the Galilean location of the first appearance to Peter.

D Two on the Emmaus Road, vv. 13–33

[13]Now, that same day two of them were traveling to a village named Emmaus, about seven miles from Jerusalem. [14]They were engaged in conversation about all that had taken place. [15]And it so happened, during the course of their discussion, that Jesus himself approached and began to walk along with them. [16]But they couldn't recognize him.

[17]He said to them, "What were you discussing as you walked along?"

Then they paused, looking depressed. [18]One of them, named Cleopas, said to him in reply, "Are you the only visitor to Jerusalem who doesn't know what's happened there these last few days?"

[19]And he said to them, "What are you talking about?"

And they said to him, "About Jesus of Nazareth, who was a prophet powerful in word and deed in the eyes of God and all the people, [20]and about how our ranking priests and rulers turned him in to be sentenced to death, and crucified him. [21]We were hoping that he would be the one who was going to ransom Israel. And as if this weren't enough, it's been three days now since all this happened. [22]Meanwhile, some women from our group gave us quite a shock. They were at the tomb early this morning [23]and didn't find his body. They came back claiming even to have seen a vision of heavenly messengers, who said that he was alive. [24]Some of those with us went to the tomb and found it exactly as the women had described; but nobody saw him."

[25]And he said to them, "You people are so slow-witted, so reluctant to trust everything the prophets have said! [26]Wasn't the Anointed One destined to undergo these things and enter into his glory?" [27]Then, starting with Moses and all the prophets, he interpreted for them every passage of scripture that referred to himself.

[28]They had gotten close to the village to which they were going, and he acted as if he were going on. [29]But they entreated him, saying, "Stay with us; it's almost evening, the day is practically over." So he went in to stay with them.

[30]And so, as soon as he took his place at table with them, he took a loaf, and gave a blessing, broke it, and started passing it out to them. [31]Then their eyes were opened and they recognized him; and he vanished from their sight. [32]They said to each other, "Weren't our hearts burning within us

while he was talking to us on the road, and explaining the
scriptures to us?" [33]And they got up at once and returned
to Jerusalem.

Verses 22–24 repeat the story of the women at the tomb, now
in retrospect. The balance of this charming story, without parallel
elsewhere in the gospels, is thought by some scholars to be mod-
eled on Genesis 18:1–15, where Abraham entertains heavenly
messengers but is at first unaware that he does so. Hebrews 13:2
may also be a reference to the Abraham story.

E Report to the Eleven, vv. 33–35

And when they found the eleven and those with them
gathered together, [34]they said, "The Lord really has been
raised, and has appeared to Simon!" [35]Then they described
what had happened on the road, and how they came to
recognize him in the breaking of the bread.

These verses were composed by Luke as a transition to the
next story. Luke again provides retrospective references, one
to the appearance to Simon (Peter), the other to the story he
has just narrated of the appearance to the two on the road to
Emmaus. Retrospective reference appears to be a literary tech-
nique of Luke.

F Appearance to the Eleven, vv. 36–49

[36]While they were talking about this, he himself appeared
among them and says to them, "Peace be with you." [37]But
they were terrified and frightened, and figured that they
were seeing a ghost.
      [38]And he said to them, "Why are you upset? Why do
such thoughts run through your minds? [39]You can see from
my hands and my feet that it's really me. Touch me and
see—a ghost doesn't have flesh and bones as you can see
that I have."
      [41]And while for sheer joy they still didn't know what to
believe and were bewildered, he said to them, "Do you have
anything here to eat?" [42]They offered him a piece of grilled
fish, [43] and he took it and ate it in front of them.

[44]Then he said to them, "This is the message I gave you while I was still with you: everything written about me in the Law of Moses and the Prophets and the Psalms is destined to come true." [45]Then he prepared their minds to understand the scriptures. [46]He said to them, "This is what is written: the Anointed will suffer and rise from the dead on the third day. [47]And all peoples will be called on to undergo a change of heart for the forgiveness of sins, beginning from Jerusalem. [48]You are witnesses to this. [49]And be prepared: I am sending what my Father promised down on you. Stay here in the city until you are invested with power from on high."

This story in Luke replaces the appearance to the eleven on a mountain in Galilee found in Matthew. Luke confines the appearances of the risen Jesus to Jerusalem and environs; Mark and Matthew locate the appearances in Galilee.

According to Reginald Fuller, the earliest appearances of Jesus were those of the exalted Christ in heaven—a luminous figure emanating the radiance of a heavenly messenger. These were gradually transformed into appearances of a resuscitated earthly figure who must subsequently ascend into heaven, a change requiring the ascension as a distinct event. Luke's version of the appearance to the eleven represents a rather advanced stage of that transformation.

G Ascension, vv. 50–53

[50]Then he led them out as far as Bethany, and lifting up his hands he blessed them. [51]And while he was blessing them, it so happened that he parted from them, and was carried up into the sky. [52]And they paid homage to him and returned to Jerusalem full of joy, [53]and were continually in the temple blessing God.

Rather than Matthew's ascent from a mountain in Galilee, Luke has Jesus ascend from Bethany, which is located on the ridge to the east of Jerusalem. Luke will repeat the ascension in the opening chapter of Acts and prepare the eleven for Pentecost, something he has already anticipated in v. 49.

6   Acts 1:1–11

Ascension

In my first book, Dear Theophilus, I treated everything Jesus used to do and teach [2]until the time he was taken up <into the skies>. This was after he had given instructions, under the influence of the holy spirit, to the apostles he had chosen. [3]He appeared to these <apostles> and gave ample proof that he was alive following his death. He appeared to them repeatedly during a forty-day period and spoke of God's domain. [4]During these appearances, he instructed them not to leave Jerusalem, but to wait for what the Father promised, as I told you: [5]"John baptized with water, but before many days you will be baptized with holy spirit."

[6]Those who had assembled kept asking him, "Lord, are you going to reestablish the kingdom of Israel at this time?"

[7]He responded to them: "We are not to know the dates or the occasions that the Father has reserved for his own decision. [8]However, you will be empowered when the holy spirit descends upon you, and you will be witnesses for me in Jerusalem, then in the whole of Judea and Samaria, and finally to the ends of the earth."

[9]When he had finished speaking, and while they were still watching him, he was lifted up and a cloud hid him from sight. [10]As they watched him disappear into the sky, suddenly two men in gleaming white apparel appeared at their side [11]and said, "Galileans, why are you standing there gazing up into the sky? This Jesus who was just taken up from you into the sky will come again just as you have seen him go."

The earliest versions of the resurrection represent the resurrection and ascension as a single event; the appearances of the risen Lord are thus appearances of a heavenly figure, as in the representations of Acts 7 (Stephen's vision) and Revelation 1. Luke's account in Luke 24 locates the ascension on the first Sunday and thus is a more primitive form; in the Acts version, a forty-day period separates the two events. However, we should probably understand both the third day and the forty-day interval as representing symbolic numbers and therefore not to be taken literally.

Also, in Luke 24 the ascension takes place in Bethany; in Acts (1:12) it occurs on the Mount of Olives. A minor discrepancy, to be sure, since the Mount of Olives is on the way to Bethany.

In these opening paragraphs of Acts, Luke sets out his overview of things: the disciples are to wait for the descent of holy spirit at Pentecost. Empowered by that spirit they will be able to proclaim the gospel in every tongue to every nation. Finally, Jesus' departure will be followed by his eventual return in the same manner: the first coming will be followed by a second coming. That is Luke's theology in a nutshell.

7   John 20:1–31

A Events at the Tomb, vv. 1–13

On Sunday, by the half-light of early morning, Mary of Magdala comes to the tomb—and sees that the stone has been moved away. [2]So she runs and comes to Simon Peter and the other disciple—the one Jesus loved most—and tells them, "They've taken the Master from the tomb, and we don't know where they've put him."

[3]So Peter and the other disciple went out, and they make their way to the tomb. [4]The two of them were running along together, but the other disciple ran faster than Peter and was the first to reach the tomb. [5]Stooping down, he could see the strips of burial cloth lying there; but he didn't go in. [6]Then Simon Peter comes along behind him and went in. He too sees the strips of burial cloth there, and also the cloth they had used to cover his head, lying not with the strips of burial cloth but rolled up by itself. [8]Then the other disciple, who had been the first to reach the tomb, came in. He saw all this, and he believed. [9]But since neither of them yet understood the prophecy that he was destined to rise from the dead, [10]these disciples went back home.

[11]Mary, however, stood crying outside, and in her tears she stooped to look into the tomb, [12]and she sees two heavenly messengers in white seated where Jesus' body had lain, one at the head and the other at the feet.

[13]"Woman, why are you crying?" they ask her.

"They've taken my Master away," she tells them, "and I don't know where they've put him."

Verses 1–2 and 11–13 are the story of Mary of Magdala's visit to the tomb on Sunday morning. In this version there is only one woman. Into this story the author has inserted the visit of Peter and "the other disciple" to the tomb. The function of this insertion is to elevate "the other disciple" to Peter's level in the struggle for ascendancy in the community. The story is clearly intrusive, since in v. 11 we return to Mary still at the tomb as though nothing had happened since v. 2, and she makes her report to the disciples in v. 18.

B The Appearance to Mary of Magdala, vv. 14–18

[14]No sooner had she said this than she turned around and sees Jesus standing there—but she didn't know that it was Jesus.

[15]"Woman," Jesus says to her, "why are you crying? Who is it you're looking for?"

She could only suppose that it was the gardener, and so she says to him, "Please, mister, if you've moved him, tell me where you've put him so I can take him away."

[16]"Mary," says Jesus.

She turns around and exclaims in Hebrew, "Rabbi!" (which means "Teacher").

[17]"Don't touch me," Jesus tells her, "because I have not yet gone back to the Father. But go to my brothers and tell them this: I'm going back to my Father and your Father— to my God and your God.'"

[18]Mary of Magdala goes and reports to the disciples, "I have seen the Master," and relates everything he had told her.

As in Matthew 28:8–10, Jesus appears to one or more women just as they are leaving the tomb. Reginald Fuller, among others, thinks the appearances to the women at the tomb have been created out of what were originally appearances of heavenly messengers (angelophanies become christophanies). In any case, it is difficult to reconcile this report with the claim reported by both Paul and Luke that Jesus appeared first to Peter.

C The Appearance to the Disciples, vv. 19–23

[19]That Sunday evening, the disciples had locked the doors for fear of the Judeans, but Jesus came and stood in front of them and he greets them: "Peace."

[20]Then he showed them his hands and his side. The disciples were delighted to see the Master. [21]Jesus greets them again: "Peace," he says. "Just as the Father sent me, so now I'm sending you."

[22]And at this he breathed over them and says, "Here's some holy spirit. Take it. [23]If you forgive anyone their sins, they are forgiven; if you do not release them from their sins, they are not released."

This appearance, which corresponds in its main features to the one narrated in Luke 24:36–49, locates the gathering of the eleven in Jerusalem, in contrast to Matthew, who locates it in Galilee. The setting is a commissioning scene: Jesus gives the spirit to the disciples and authorizes them to carry on in his name.

D Doubting Thomas, vv. 24–29

[24]Now Thomas, the one known as "the Twin," one of the twelve, hadn't been with them when Jesus put in his appearance. [25]So the other disciples tried to tell him, "We've seen the Master."

But he responded, "Unless I see the holes the nails made, and put my finger in them and my hand in his side, I'll never believe."

[26]A week later the disciples were again indoors, and Thomas was with them. The doors were locked, but Jesus comes and stood in front of them, and said, "Peace." [27]Then he says to Thomas, "Put your finger here, and look at my hands; take your hand and put it in my side. Don't be skeptical but be a believer."

[28]Thomas responded, "My Master! My God!"

[29]"Do you believe because you have seen me?" asks Jesus. "Those who can believe without having to see are the ones to be congratulated."

This story is unique among appearance stories. It stands in tension with the preceding narrative, in which presumably all the disciples, including Thomas, were present. This story represents the ultimate attempt to historicize the appearances of the risen Jesus by including physically palpable narrative elements.

E Conclusion, vv. 30–31

[30]Although Jesus performed many more miracles for his disciples to see than could be written down in this book, [31]these are written so you will come to believe that Jesus is the Anointed, God's son—and by believing this have life in his name.

These verses, which function as a concluding statement, are proof that the Gospel of John originally ended with chapter 20.

8   John 21:1–23

A Appearance to Peter and the Six, vv. 1–14

Some time after these events, Jesus again appeared to his disciples by the Sea of Tiberias. This is how he did it: [2]When Simon Peter and Thomas, the one known as "the Twin," were together, along with Nathaniel from Cana, Galilee, the sons of Zebedee, and two other disciples, [3]Simon Peter says to them, "I'm going to go fishing."

"We're coming with you," they reply.

They went down and got into the boat, but that night they didn't catch a thing.

[4]It was already getting light when Jesus appeared on the shore, but his disciples didn't recognize that it was Jesus. [5]"Lads, you haven't caught any fish, have you?" Jesus asks them. "No," they replied.

[6]He tells them, "Cast your net on the right side of the boat and you'll have better luck."

They do as he instructs them and now they can't haul it in for the huge number of fish. [7]The disciple Jesus loved most exclaims to Peter, "It's the Master!"

When Simon Peter heard "It's the Master," he tied his cloak around himself, since he was stripped for work, and threw himself into the water. [8]The rest of them came in the boat, dragging the net full of fish. They were not far from land, only about a hundred yards offshore.

[9]When they got to shore, they see a charcoal fire burning, with fish cooking on it, and some bread. [10]Jesus says to them, "Bring some of the fish you've just caught."

[11]Then Simon Peter went aboard and hauled the net full of large fish ashore—one hundred fifty-three of them. Even though there were so many of them, the net still didn't tear.

[12]Jesus says to them, "Come and eat."

None of the disciples dared ask, "Who are you?" They knew it was the Master. [13]Jesus comes, takes the bread and gives it to them, and passes the fish around as well.

[14]This was now the third time after he had been raised from the dead that Jesus appeared to his disciples.

The similarities of this story to the call of Peter in Luke 5:1–11 have often been noted. There are seven disciples in this case, which probably symbolizes the future church, since seven is the number of perfection. Once again, the disciple whom Jesus loved most recognizes Jesus before Peter (v. 7). The miraculous catch of fish—153 in number—in all probability refers to the unlimited success of the Christian mission. And, once again, a resurrection appearance is linked to the breaking of bread (note Luke 24, the two on the road to Emmaus).

B Admonition to Peter, vv. 15–23

[15]When they had eaten, Jesus asks Simon Peter, "Simon, John's son, do you love me more than they do?"

"Of course, Master; you know I love you," he replies.

"Then keep feeding my lambs," Jesus tells him.

[16]<Jesus> asks him again, for the second time, "Simon, John's son, do you love me?"

"Yes, Master; you know I love you," he replies.

"Keep shepherding my sheep."

[17]<Jesus> says to him a third time, "Simon, John's son, do you love me?"

Peter was hurt that he had asked him for the third time, "Do you love me?" and he says to him, "Master, you know everything; you know I love you."

Jesus says to him, "Keep feeding my sheep. [18]I swear to God, when you were young you used to gather your cloak about you and go where you wanted to go. But when you've grown old, you'll stretch out your arms, and someone else will get you ready and take you where you don't want to go."

([19]He said this to indicate with what kind of death <Peter> would honor God.)

And after saying this, he adds, "Keep following me."

[20]Peter turns and sees the disciple Jesus loved most following them—the one who had leaned over on Jesus' right at supper and asked, "Master, who is going to turn you in?" [21]When Peter saw this disciple <following>, he asks Jesus, "Master, what about this fellow?"

[22]Jesus replies to him, "What business is it of yours if I want him to stay around till I come? You are to keep on following me."

([23]Because of this the rumor spread among the family of believers that this disciple wouldn't die. But Jesus had not said to him, "He won't die"; he said, "What business is it of yours if I want him to stay around till I come?")

This story depicts the rehabilitation of Peter and restores his pre-eminent position. Peter had denied Jesus at his trial, but then was the first to identify Jesus as the risen lord. Jesus once again commissions Peter to head up the new movement.

9   Gospel of Peter 9–14

The Resurrection

9 Early, at first light on the sabbath, a crowd came from
Jerusalem and the surrounding countryside to see the sealed
tomb. [2]But during the night before the Lord's day dawned,
while the soldiers were on guard, two by two during each
watch, a loud noise came from the sky, [3]and they saw the
skies open up and two men come down from there in a
burst of light and approach the tomb. [4]The stone that had
been pushed against the entrance began to roll by itself and
moved away to one side; then the tomb opened up and
both youths went inside.

10 Now when these soldiers saw this, they roused the
centurion from his sleep, along with the elders—remember,
they were also there keeping watch. [2]While they were
explaining what they had seen, again they see three men
leaving the tomb, two supporting the third, and a cross
was following them. [3]The heads of the two reached up to
the sky, while the head of the third, whom they led by the
hand, reached beyond the skies. [4]And they heard a voice
from the skies that said, "Have you preached to those who
sleep?" [5]And an answer was heard from the cross: "Yes!"

11 These men then consulted with one another about
going and reporting these things to Pilate. [2]While they
were still thinking about it, again the skies appeared to open
and some sort of human being came down and entered
the tomb. [3]When those in the centurion's company saw
this, they rushed out into the night to Pilate, having left
the tomb which they were supposed to be guarding. And
as they were recounting everything they had seen, they
became deeply disturbed and cried, "Truly, he was a son of
God!"

[4]Pilate responded by saying, "I am clean of the blood of
the son of God; this was all your doing."

[5]Then they all crowded around <Pilate> and began to
beg and urge him to order the centurion and his soldiers to
tell no one what they saw. [6]"You see," they said, "it is better
for us to be guilty of the greatest sin before God than to fall

into the hands of the Jewish people and be stoned." [7]Pilate
then ordered the centurion and the soldiers to say nothing.

12 Early on the Lord's day, Mary of Magdala, a disciple of
the Lord was fearful on account of the Jews, and since they
were enflamed with rage, she did not perform at the tomb
of the Lord what women are accustomed to do for their
beloved who die. [2]Nevertheless, she took her friends with
her and went to the tomb where he had been laid. [3]And
they were afraid that the Jews might see them and were saying, "Although on the day he was crucified we could not
weep and beat our breasts, we should now perform these
rites at his tomb. [4]But who will roll away the stone for us,
the one placed at the entrance of the tomb, so that we may
enter and sit beside him and do what ought to be done?"
[5](Remember, it was a huge stone.) "We fear that someone
might see us. And if we are unable <to roll the stone away>
we should, at least, place at the entrance the memorial we
brought for him, and we should weep and beat our breasts
until we go home."

13 And they went and found the tomb open. They
went up to it, stooped down, and saw a youth sitting there
<in> the middle of the tomb; he was handsome and wore
a splendid robe. He said to them, [2]"Why have you come?
Who are you looking for? Surely not the one who was crucified? He is risen and gone. If you don't believe it, stoop
down and take a look at the place where he lay, for he is
not there. You see, he is risen and has gone back to the
place he was sent from." [3]Then the women fled in fear.

14 Now it was the last day of Unleavened Bread, and
many began to return to their homes since the feast was
over. [2]But we, the twelve disciples of the Lord, continued to
weep and mourn, and each one, still grieving on account of
what had happened, left for his own home. [3]But I, Simon
Peter, and Andrew, my brother, took our fishing nets and
went away to the sea. And with us was Levi, the son of
Alphaeus, whom the Lord . . .

A fragment of the Gospel of Peter was discovered in 1886 by a group of French archaeologists at work in Egypt. Two additional small pieces belonging to the same scroll were published in 1972 as Oxyrhynchus fragment 2949. The first, longer text was copied in all probability in the seventh or eighth century; the second fragments can be dated to the late second or early third centuries. The textual evidence for the existence of the Gospel of Peter is thus as old as that for either Matthew or Luke.

What makes Peter of special interest is the depiction of the resurrection in chapters 9 and 10. There a loud noise is heard from the skies and two figures descend in a burst of light and enter the tomb. They reappear supporting a third figure between them, whose head reached beyond the skies; the two side figures were as tall as the sky. A cross followed the trio. A voice from the skies then inquires whether "you" have preached to the dead. A positive response comes from the cross, not from any of the figures.

It is possible that the cross symbolizes the righteous ones of Israel who have suffered unjustly. The redeemer figure has freed them from the chains of Sheol to share in the general resurrection here suggested.

This narration of events is so generalized and fits so well with older Israelite traditions that Dominic Crossan has argued that the Gospel of Peter is the oldest account of the death and resurrection of Jesus and is the ultimate source of all four canonical accounts. Other scholars insist that Peter instead represents a summary and elaboration of the New Testament gospels.

10 Gospel of the Hebrews 9

The Appearance to James

The Lord, after he had given the linen cloth to
the priest's slave, sent to James and appeared to
him. [2](Now James had sworn not to eat bread
from the time that he drank from the Lord's cup
until he would see him raised from among those
who sleep.)
[3]Shortly after this the Lord said, "Bring a table and some
bread."
[4]And immediately it is added:
He took the bread, blessed it, broke it, and gave
it to James the Just and said to him, "My brother,
eat your bread, for the Son of Adam has been
raised from among those who sleep."

This fragment of the Gospel of the Hebrews was cited by
Jerome, a Christian scholar of the fourth to fifth centuries. It
identifies James, the brother of Jesus, as the first to witness the
resurrection rather than Peter or Mary of Magdala. It also represents James as having taken a vow to fast until the resurrection
occurs. In Luke 22:16 it is Jesus who vows to fast—until the
kingdom arrives.

11 Pseudo-Mark 16:9–20

Two Appearances to Mary in the Country, and One to the Eleven

[9]Now after he arose at daybreak on Sunday, he appeared first to Mary of Magdala, from whom he had driven out seven demons. [10]She went and told those who were close to him, who were mourning and weeping. [11]But when those folks heard that he was alive and had been seen by her, they did not believe it.

[12]A little later he appeared to two of them in a different guise as they were walking along, on their way to the country. [13]And these two returned and told the others. They did not believe them either.

[14]Later he appeared to the eleven as they were reclining <at a meal>. He reproached them for their lack of trust and obstinacy, because they did not believe those who had seen him after he had been raised. [15]And he said to them: "Go out into the whole world and announce the good news to every creature. [16]Whoever trusts and is baptized will be saved. The one who lacks trust will be condemned. [17]These are the signs that will accompany those who have trust: they will drive out demons in my name; they will speak in new tongues; [18]they will pick up snakes with their hands; and even if they swallow poison, it certainly won't harm them; they will lay their hands on those who are sick, and they will get well."

[19]The Lord Jesus, after he said these things, was taken up into the sky and sat down at the right hand of God. [20]Those <to whom he had spoken> went out and made their announcement everywhere, and the Lord worked with them and certified what they said by means of accompanying signs.

Many early scribes felt that the Gospel of Mark was not complete. Accordingly, they provided endings to Mark, of which two have survived. The longer of them, translated here, is usually versified as Mark 16:9–20.

Three appearances are narrated: to Mary of Magdala, to two walking along toward the country, and to the eleven as they were eating. The appearances are followed by a commission and by the ascension.

This summary appears to be based on the Gospel of Luke; it is also possible that the post-resurrection narrative in the Gospel of Luke is an elaboration of this outline.

12 The Transfiguration (Three Versions)

A Mark 9:2–8

²Six days later, Jesus takes Peter and James and John along and leads them off by themselves to a lofty mountain. He was transformed in front of them, ³and his clothes became an intensely brilliant white, whiter than any laundry on earth could make them. ⁴Elijiah appeared to them, with Moses, and they were conversing with Jesus. ⁵ Peter responds by saying to Jesus, "Rabbi, it's a good thing we're here. In fact, why not set up three tents, one for you, and one for a Moses, and one for Elijah!" (⁶you see, he didn't know how else to respond, since they were terrified.)

⁷And a cloud moved in and cast a shadow over them, and a voice came out of the cloud: "This is my favorite son, listen to him!" ⁸Suddenly, as they looked around, they saw no one, but were alone with Jesus.

B Matthew 17:1–8

Six days later, Jesus takes Peter and James and his brother John along and he leads them off by themselves to a lofty mountain. ²He was transformed in front of them and his face shone like the sun, and his clothes turned as white as light. ³The next thing you know, Moses and Elijah appeared to them and were conversing with Jesus.

⁴Then Peter responded by saying to Jesus, "Master, it's a good thing we're here. If you want, I'll set up three tents here, one for you, one for Moses, and one for Elijah!"

⁵While he was still speaking, there was a bright cloud that cast a shadow over them. And just then a voice spoke from the cloud: "This is my favored son of whom I fully approve. Listen to him!"

⁶And as the disciples listened, they prostrated themselves, and were frightened out of their wits.

⁷And Jesus came and touched them and said: "Get up; don't be afraid." ⁸Looking up they saw no one except Jesus by himself.

C Luke 9:28–36

[28]About eight days after these sayings, Jesus happened to take Peter and John and James along with him and climbed up the mountain to pray. [29]And it so happened as he was praying that his face took on a strange appearance, and his clothing turned dazzling white. [30]The next thing you know, two figures were talking with him, Moses and Elijah, [31]who appeared in glory and were discussing his departure, which he was destined to carry out in Jerusalem. [32]Now Peter and those with him were half asleep at the time. But they came wide awake when they saw his glory and the two men standing next to him. [33]And it so happened as the men were leaving him that Peter said to Jesus, "Master, it's a good thing we're here. In fact, why not set up three tents, one for you, one for Moses, and one for Elijah!" (He didn't know what he was saying). [34]While he was still speaking, a cloud moved in and cast a shadow over them. And their fear increased as they entered the cloud. [35]And out of the cloud a voice spoke: "This is my son, my chosen one. Listen to him!" [36]When the voice had spoken, Jesus was perceived to be alone. And they were speechless and told no one back then anything of what they had seen.

If the original appearance stories visualized the risen Jesus as a luminous heavenly body, the transfiguration story may well be a variant on that theme. The luminous tradition incorporates two themes, the dazzling light, often at midday, and a communication by voice. Those two characteristics also appear in this story.

On the assumption that the transfiguration story was originally an appearance story, it has been remodeled along the lines of the baptismal story, except that here Jesus is transfigured as a heavenly body, like that of an angel. But there is a voice out of the cloud—concealed as it were, because no one can look on the radiance of God without being blinded—that identifies who Jesus is. As in the baptismal story, the voice from heaven is a theophany.

The two figures that appear here with Jesus—Moses and Elijah—parallel the twin heavenly figures that appear in the Gospel of Peter 9–10 and Luke 24:4.

13 Luke 5:1–11

The Miraculous Catch of Fish

On one occasion, when the crowd pressed him to hear the word of God, he was standing by the lake of Gennesaret. [2]He noticed two boats moored there at the shore; the fishermen had left them and were washing their nets. [3]He got into one of the boats, the one belonging to Simon, and asked him to put out a little from the shore. Then he sat down and began to teach the crowds from the boat.

[4]When he had finished speaking, he said to Simon, "Put out into deep water and lower your nets for a catch."

[5]But Simon replied, "Master, we've been hard at it all night and haven't caught a thing. But if you insist, I'll lower the nets."

[6]So they did and netted such a huge number of fish that their nets began to tear apart. [7]They signaled to their partners in the other boat to come and lend a hand. They came and loaded both boats until they nearly sank.

[8]At the sight of this, Simon Peter fell to his knees in front of Jesus and said, "Have nothing to do with me, Master, heathen that I am." [9]For he and his companions were stunned at the catch of fish they had taken, [10]as were James and John, sons of Zebedee and partners of Simon.

Jesus said to Simon, "Don't be afraid; from now on you'll be catching people." [11]They then brought their boats to shore, abandoned everything, and followed him.

The story of the miraculous catch of fish in Luke 5:1–11 has five noteworthy parallels with the story in John 21:

- In both there is an unsuccessful fishing trip
- In both there are allusions to Peter's denial
- In both there is a miraculous catch
- Both are call stories
- In both Peter is the leading figure. These are the reasons many scholars have concluded that Luke 5:1–11 and John 21 are versions of the same story. If so, we have important evidence that the evangelists felt free to relocate appearances of the risen Jesus.

14 Paul's Vision on the Damascus Road (Three Versions)

A Acts 9:3–19

³As Saul was traveling along and getting close to Damascus, he was suddenly dazzled by a light emanating from the sky. ⁴He fell to the ground and heard a voice saying to him, "Saul, Saul, why are you persecuting me?"

⁵Saul replied, "Who are you, lord?"

The voice continued, "The one you are persecuting is Jesus. ⁶Get up and go into town. You will be told what you have to do." ⁷Saul's traveling companions stood by dumbfounded; they had heard the voice but said nothing. ⁸Saul picked himself up from the ground but when he opened his eyes he was unable to see anything. His companions took him by the hand and led him into Damascus. ⁹For three days he was blind and neither ate nor drank.

¹⁰There was this disciple in Damascus named Ananias. The lord called to him in a vision, "Ananias," it said.

He replied, "It's me, my lord."

¹¹The lord instructed him, "Get up and go to Straight Street. Ask for Saul of Tarsus in the home of Judas. You should understand that he is currently praying; ¹²he has had a vision of someone named Ananias coming in and laying hands on him so he can see."

¹³Ananias replied, "Lord, many people have told me about this man and reported the wicked treatment he has given your followers in Jerusalem. ¹⁴And here <in Damascus> he has been authorized by the high priest to arrest everyone who claims your name."

¹⁵The lord responded to Ananias, "Go anyway. This fellow is a special instrument of mine to champion my cause in front of heathen and their royalty and before the people of Israel. ¹⁶Understand, I intend to show him how much he has to suffer for my sake."

¹⁷So Ananias went, entered the house, and placed his hands on Saul: "Saul, my brother," he said, "the lord Jesus who appeared to you on your way here has sent me so you may recover your sight and be filled with holy spirit." ¹⁸Instantly something like scales fell from his eyes so he

could see again. He got up and was baptized. [19]Then he ate something to get his strength back.

B Acts 22 :1–16

"Friends and distinguished elders, listen, please, to the defense I now plead before you."

[2]When they heard him address them in Hebrew, they quieted down.

[3]Paul went on: "I am a Jew I was born in Tarsus, Cilicia. I was raised here in Jerusalem. I was trained by Gamaliel in the fine points of our ancestral law. I was a zealot in my devotion to God, just as you are on this occasion. [4]I persecuted this movement to the death, arresting men and women alike and turning them over to the jailer. [5]The chief priest and the Council of Elders can testify to this. From them I received written authorization to our associates in Damascus. I was on my way there to get prisoners also and bring them to Jerusalem for punishment.

[6]"As I was going along, this is what happened to me as I got near Damascus, about noon: an intense light from the sky engulfed me. [7]I fell to the ground and I heard a voice speaking to me, 'Saul, Saul, why are you persecuting me?'

[8]"I replied, 'Who are you, lord?'

"He said to me, 'The one you are persecuting is Jesus the Nazarene.'

[9]"My traveling companions saw the light but did not hear a voice speaking to me. [10]I asked, 'What should I do, Lord?'

"The Lord replied to me, 'Get up and go into Damascus. There you will be told everything you have to do.'

[11]"Since I could not see as a consequence of the dazzling light, my companions took me by the hand and led me into Damascus.

[12]"Ananias was a devout person by the standards of the law and all the Jewish inhabitants of Damascus thought well of him. [13] He came and stood before me and declared, 'Saul, my friend, you have your sight back again!' At that precise moment I opened my eyes and there he was. [14]"He then told me, 'Our ancestral God has destined you to know his will, to lay eyes on the righteous one, and to hear the latter speak. [15]On his behalf you are to testify to the whole world,

to everything you have seen and heard. [16]And now why do you hesitate? Get going and get baptized to wash away your sins by invoking his name."

C Acts 26:9–18

[9]"I myself considered it my duty to do as much as I could in opposing the name of Jesus of Nazareth, [10]and that's what I did in Jerusalem. I clamped many members of the movement in prison on the authority of the chief priests, and I concurred in their condemnation by casting my <black> pebble against them. [11]I would frequently punish them in all the synagogues and try to make them blaspheme. And in my fury I even pursued them to foreign cities.

[12]"While I was on my way to Damascus on the authority and with the approval of the chief priests, [13]along the road, about noon, your majesty, I saw a light emanating from the sky, whose brilliance exceeded that of the sun. It engulfed me and my traveling companions. [14]All of us dropped to the ground, and I heard a voice speaking to me in Hebrew, 'Saul, Saul,' it said, why are you persecuting me? You are bringing pain on yourself by resisting the prod.'

[15]"Then I said, 'Who are you, lord?'

"He replied, 'The one you are persecuting is Jesus. [16]But get up on your feet. The reason I have appeared to you is to commission you as my servant and as a witness to the things you have seen and to the appearances I will yet make to you. [17]I will rescue you from your own people, and from the gentiles, to whom I am sending you, [18]to open their eyes so they will turn from darkness to light, and from the power of Satan to God. They will then have their sins forgiven and find a place among those God has made his own through faith in me.'"

The overarching question for scholars is whether these three accounts of Paul's vision on the Damascus road are accurate depictions of the appearance to which Paul lays claim in 1 Corinthians 15:8. Paul believes he was appointed an apostle directly by the authority of the risen Jesus; Luke, however, demotes Paul from the circle of the twelve even though he pictures Paul as his hero. For Luke only someone who accompanied

Jesus during his earthly ministry can be an apostle (Acts 13:31), presumably because only Jesus' friends would recognize him in his risen state. It is also a question of authority: the witnesses of the resurrection are those who are in authority.

There are some inconsistencies in the three versions of the event described by Luke. They agree that there was a bright light and a voice from the skies, but they do not agree about who heard and saw on each occasion. It is necessary to bear in mind that storytellers the world over are not incapable of giving alternative descriptions or explanations for the same events or series of events. To this common practice Luke is no exception. We do him and others an injustice by forcing them to meet our standards for consistency in narration, whether fictive or historical.

15 Acts 7:55–56

Vision of Stephen

[55]But Stephen, who was filled with holy spirit, looked up into the sky and saw the effulgence of God and Jesus standing on the right side of God. [56]He said, "Here I am looking at the sky opened up and the son of Adam standing on the right side of God."

This obviously is an account of a vision of the exalted Christ or son of Adam standing alongside God, more precisely, alongside the dazzling brilliance of God, who appears, as do God's messengers, as a blinding light.

Luke would not count it among the appearances to those endowed with apostolic authority.

16 Revelation 1:13–16

Vision of John on Patmos

¹³Among the lampstands [I saw] a figure that looked like a human being. He had on a full length robe and a golden sash around his chest. ¹⁴His head and hair were white as wool can get, as white as snow, and his eyes flashed like fire; ¹⁵his feet had the appearance of polished bronze that had been refined in a smelter; his voice sounded like a mighty torrent tumbling down. ¹⁶He held seven stars in his right hand and a sharp double-edged sword jutted from his mouth. His face was as radiant as the naked sun.

Heavenly figures that look like human beings (v. 13) are being distinguished from heavenly figures that look like animals, such as the beast with seven heads and ten horns in Revelation 17, and the son of Adam and the beasts in Daniel 7. Here, too, the redeemer figure is compared to the whitest thing on earth and to the naked sun in brilliance. His voice is like thunder. This vision, like its counterparts, is depicted entirely in traditional terms.

Conclusion

Readers now have before them all the primary texts, together with a brief commentary on each of them. The two key questions are these: How will the Jesus Seminar color code each of the texts, and what reasons will the Seminar advance for the color decisions it makes?

Chapter Two

The Jesus Seminar Spring Meeting 1995

A t the Spring 1995 meeting, the Fellows and Associates faced some of the most controversial topics in biblical literature—including the resurrection of Jesus.

Forty-five scholars debated and voted on the narratives surrounding the resurrection, including the burial and appearances.

What Happened to the Corpse of Jesus?

Prof. Luedemann of the University of Gottingen, Germany, argued in a public address that the body of Jesus undoubtedly decayed in the usual way. The Fellows approved this thesis overwhelmingly. They found that Jesus' corpse probably rotted in some unknown grave, a view supported by most Associate members. More than ninety percent of the Fellows, and a huge majority of Associates, agreed that Jesus' resurrection did not involve the resuscitation of his corpse.

In related deliberation and voting, it was the unanimous judgment of the Fellows that belief in Jesus' resurrection did not depend on what happened to his corpse.

The Fourth R 8,2 (March/April 1995), pp. 10–11

Appearances

Paul, Mary of Magdala, Peter, and possibly others in the early Jesus movement experienced visions of a glorified Jesus, which they interpreted as evidence of his resurrection.

The earliest reports of Jesus' appearances were of luminous apparitions—a blinding light—accompanied by some auditory communication (real or imagined). The Fellows, along with many other critical scholars, view the empty tomb story as a legend that developed three or four decades after Jesus' death—probably in response to the rumor that Jesus' followers had stolen his body.

In probing the issues surrounding the resurrection, the Fellows agreed that Jesus' resurrection was not an event open to empirical verification. As Prof. Marcus Borg of Oregon State University put it, "a video camera present at one of Jesus' appearances would not have recorded anything on tape." Associates concurred in this judgment.

Burial

The Jesus Seminar concluded that Jesus' body was probably disposed of by his enemies, rather than by his friends. He may not have been buried at all, but left to the mercy of the elements or to scavenging dogs—often the practice in Roman executions. In either case, Jesus' disciples did not know what happened to the body.

The account of the empty tomb found in the last chapter of the Gospel of Mark is a late legend, introduced into the tradition for the first time by Mark. Or, in the opinion of John Dominic Crossan of DePaul University, the empty tomb was introduced for the first time by the Gospel of Peter, on which Mark's story is based. In either case, it does not rest on historical memory.

The Fellows are inclined to the view that Joseph of Arimathea was a fictional character. Those Fellows who think Joseph was not a fiction doubt that he was a disciple of Jesus and Jesus' undertaker.

Location of the Appearances

Most Fellows believe that the earliest apparitions of Jesus took place in Galilee, as forecast in the Gospel of Mark and depicted by Matthew (dependent on Mark). This detail alone makes it very difficult to believe that the appearances reported in Luke—all of which are located in or around Jerusalem—are historically accurate. Indeed, Luke has Jesus command the disciples to remain in Jerusalem—probably to soften the story that the disciples had forsaken Jesus during his trial and fled. The Gospel of John reports appearances in both locations, but places the Jerusalem stories before the appearances in Galilee—a very unlikely sequence.

How Long Did Easter Last?

Various claims of appearances make it difficult to say how long Easter lasted. Visionary experiences of Jesus are reported to have gone on for months, perhaps even years.

The appearance to Paul of Tarsus, for example, must have taken place three or four years after the crucifixion, not in the forty days following Easter. In his gospel, Luke reports that Jesus ascended to heaven on Easter Sunday evening, but then has Jesus tarry on earth for forty days in the opening paragraphs of the book of Acts. Secret James, a book found in the Nag Hammadi library, has Jesus continue his instruction of the disciples for 550 days. The Pistis Sophia, a collection of writings emanating from Egypt in the third century, represents Jesus as prolonging his instruction of certain followers for eleven years. And reported sightings of Jesus continue, even into twentieth century America.

Visionary Religious Experiences

The Fellows were fairly confident that both Peter and Paul had visions of the luminous Christ figure, as Paul reports in 1 Corinthians 15 and Luke confirms in his gospel (24:34). But the Fellows tended to be skeptical about the claims made on behalf of James and John (sons of Zebedee), James the brother of Jesus, "the twelve," all the apostles, and the 500 who presumably had a simultaneous group experience (1 Cor 15:5–8).

If Peter's vision is narrated anywhere in the New Testament gospels, it is probably preserved indirectly in the story of the miraculous catch of fish in Luke 5:1–11. This account may well be a misplaced appearance story.

James M. Robinson of the Institute for Antiquity and
Christianity, Claremont, California, formulated a general statement that the depiction of the resurrection appearances found
at the end of the New Testament gospels are late and secondary.
With this the Seminar agrees. The earlier form of appearance was
the luminous vision—the blinding light, like that which Luke
attributes to Paul in the book of Acts (9:1–19). Later, as the tradition developed, the reported experiences became more and more
palpable—physical, flesh-and-blood appearances.

This later view was in contrast to the earlier, more spiritual
view of the resurrection. In concert with this affirmation, the
Fellows concluded that claims of Jesus' resurrection are statements
of faith, not reports of an historical event or events.

The Tomb

All the reports of the tomb—the empty tomb, the appearances
of angels at or near the tomb, the appearances of the risen Jesus
at the tomb—were voted black by the Fellows (that is, the stories are not reports of historical events). The sole exception is the
report in John 20:1–2 that Mary of Magdala came to the tomb
and found it empty. This was voted gray, suggesting that some
aspect of the story may reflect a historical reminiscence.

While the Fellows believe the empty tomb story is secondary
and fictional, they think Mary's role in events has been partially
suppressed. In the Gospel of Mary (7:1), she claims to have had
her own vision of the risen lord. But she is not mentioned, for
example, in Paul's list of appearance witnesses in 1 Corinthians.
In the view of the Seminar scholars, she would have been mentioned had she not been a woman.

Chapter Three

Brand X Easters

Robert M. Price

We begin the process of becoming critical readers of the Bible the first time we are dissatisfied with being told what the text means and decide to see for ourselves. And we soon discover that there really is no alternative to reading the text for ourselves. We may listen to and read many opinions—the more the better, in fact—but ultimately it is up to us. We must give the text our own careful scrutiny to see what it means.

Likewise, one frequently reads generalizations about ancient texts, and may at first be willing to assume the experts are assessing the evidence correctly. But as soon as we become aware of scholarly debates on, for example, whether ancient Gnostics really believed in a divine redeemer, or dying and rising saviors were a dime a dozen in antiquity, well, that is when it strikes us: we have to scrutinize all *those* texts for ourselves! It seems one simply cannot hold serious scholarly opinions second hand. I have assured readers more than once that the resurrection stories of the New Testament are cut from the same cloth as many others from the same environment. But I don't want anyone to take my word for it. Let's put the cards on the table, shall we?

Without a Trace

Many readers have wondered how Mark could possibly have been satisfied to end his gospel without resurrection appearances. But Charles H. Talbert, in his groundbreaking *What Is a Gospel?*,

---

The Fourth R 20,6 (November/December 2007), 13–19, 23

demonstrated what Mark was probably thinking. He showed how many ancient Hellenistic texts tell the story of a divine hero's exaltation to heaven. Some exaltations were followed by visions of the departed savior, others not. It sufficed that the hero's followers seek his missing or slain body, find no trace of clothing or flesh, and finally be assured by a heavenly voice or visitor that he had been taken up to heavenly glory. Nuff said!

After Herakles, son of Zeus, died, his friends looked for his bones and found nary a one. Because they recalled a prior prophecy that he was destined for immortality, they concluded he must have been taken to heaven.

> As Herakles continued to suffer more and more from his malady he sent Licymnius and Iolaüs to Delphi to inquire of Apollo what he must do to recover. The god replied that Herakles should be taken, along with his armor and weapons, to Oete and that they should build a huge pyre near him. The god said that what remained to be done would be up to Zeus.
>
> Now when Iolaüs had carried out these orders and had withdrawn to a distance to see what would take place, Herakles, having abandoned hope for himself, ascended the pyre and asked each one who came up to him to light it. No one had the courage to obey him except Philoctetes. Having received in return for his compliance the gift of the bow and arrows of Herakles, he lit the pyre. Immediately lightning fell from the heavens and the pyre was wholly consumed.
>
> After this, when the companions of Iolaüs came to gather up the bones of Herakles and found not a single bone anywhere, they assumed that, in accordance with the words of the oracle, he had passed from among men into the company of the gods. (Diodorus of Sicily, *Library of History* 4:38:3–5)

Likewise, Apollo's son Aristaeus, after dwelling in the region of Mt. Haemus, was never seen again, and all men assumed he had been taken up.

> And finally, as the myths relate, he visited Dionysus in Thrace and was initiated into his secret rites, and during his stay in the company of the god he learned from him much useful knowledge. And after dwelling some time in the

neighborhood of Mount Haemus he never was seen again by men, and became the recipient of immortal honors not only among the barbarians of that region but among the Greeks as well. (Diodorus of Sicily, *Library of History* 4.82.6)

Aeneas, son of Venus, was the survivor of Troy whose descendants founded Rome. After a certain battle, no one could find a trace of his body, so they concluded he had been raptured to the gods.

A severe battle took place not far from Lavinium and many were slain on both sides, but when night came on the armies separated; and when the body of Aeneas was nowhere to be seen, some concluded that it had been translated to the gods and others that it had perished in the river beside which the battle was fought. And the Latins built a hero-shrine to him with this inscription: "To the father and god of this place, who presides over the waters of the river Numicius." (Dionysus of Halicarnassus, *Roman Antiquities* 1.64.4–5)

Likewise, Romulus, son of Mars, vanished from human sight after a battle in which the sun was momentarily darkened. Some claimed actually to have seen him ascending from the battlefield. He was deified as the god Quirinus.

He disappeared on the Nones of July . . . leaving nothing of certainty to be related of his death: only the time . . . Romulus, when he vanished, left neither the least part of his body, nor any remnant of his clothes to be seen . . . the senators suffered them not to search, or busy themselves about the matter, but commanded them to honor and worship Romulus as one taken up to the gods. (Plutarch, *Romulus* 2:27)

Empedocles the philosopher (484–424 BCE) invited some friends to a sacrificial feast.

Then, after the feast, the remainder of the company dispersed and retired to rest . . . while Empedocles himself remained on the spot where he had reclined at table. At daybreak all got up, and he was the only one missing. A search was made and they questioned the servants, who said they did not know where he was. Thereupon someone said that in the middle of the night he heard an exceedingly loud voice calling Empedocles. Then he got up and beheld

a light in the heavens and a glitter of lamps, but nothing
else. His hearers were amazed at what had occurred, and
Pausanias came down and sent people to search for him.
But later he bade them take no further trouble, for things
beyond expectation had happened to him, and it was their
duty to sacrifice to him since he was now a god. (Diogenes
Laertius, *Lives of Eminent Philosophers* 8:68)

Apollonius of Tyana (a contemporary of Paul), son of Proteus, was
said to have entered Dictynna's temple in Crete late one night,
rousing the fearsome guard dogs. But

instead of barking, they approached him and fawned upon
him . . . The guardians of the temple arrested him in consequence, and threw him in bonds as a wizard and a robber,
accusing him of having thrown to the dogs some charmed
morsel. But about midnight he loosened his bonds, and
after calling those who had bound him, in order that they
might witness the spectacle, he ran to the doors of the temple, which opened wide to receive him; and when he had
passed within they closed afresh, as they had been shut, and
there was heard a chorus of maidens singing from within
the temple, and their song was this. "Hasten thou from
earth, hasten thou to Heaven, hasten!" He was no more
seen on earth. (Philostratus, *Life of Apollonius of Tyana* 8:30)

One particular story of the discovery of an empty tomb, dating from a little before the time of John's gospel, contains a
scene quite similar to that in John 20:1–8. It is a passage from
Chariton's *Chaireas and Kalliroe*, a novel written probably in the
first century BCE. It concerns a girl, mistakenly entombed alive,
who has been removed by grave robbers.

Chaireas was guarding and toward dawn he approached
the tomb. . . . When he came close, however, he found
the stones moved away and the entrance open. He looked
in and was shocked, seized by a great perplexity at what
had happened. Rumor made an immediate report to the
Syracusans about the miracles. All then ran to the tomb;
no one dared to enter until Hermocrates ordered it. One
was sent in and he reported everything accurately. It
seemed incredible—the dead girl was not there. . . . [When
Chaireas] searched the tomb he was able to find nothing.
Many came in after him, disbelieving. Amazement seized

everyone, and some said as they stood there: "The shroud has been stripped off, this is the work of grave robbers; but where is the body?" (Dungan and Cartlidge, 157)

I am not suggesting that John or the other evangelists used this novel as a source. I mean only to show that vivid descriptions of empty tombs and abandoned graveclothes prove nothing about "eyewitness authorship" since we find them also in an admitted work of fiction.

Postmortem Appearance and Great Commission

Matthew and Luke were not satisfied with Mark's teasing announcement of the Risen Jesus without any appearances, so they added appearances in which the vanished Jesus appears and delivers his own eulogy—summing up his mission and giving the disciples their marching orders. Such appearances, literary devices used to interpret the lasting significance of the hero for the readers, were common enough in Hellenistic religious literature, as witnessed by the following episodes in which Romulus, the legendary founder of Rome, appears after his initial lift-off from earth.

> Proculus Julius [a Roman senator] was coming from the Alba Longa; the moon was shining, he was not using a torch. Suddenly the hedges on the left shook and moved. He shrank back and his hair stood on end. Beautiful and more than human and clothed in a sacred robe, Romulus was seen, standing in the middle of the road. He said, "Stop the (Romans) from their mourning; do not let them violate my divinity with their tears; order the pious crowd to bring incense and worship the new [god] Quirinus." . . . He gave the order and he vanished into the upper world from before Julius' eyes."
>
> Julius Proculus said, "Romulus Quirites, the father of this city, at the first light of this day, descended from the sky and clearly showed himself to me. While I was awed with holy fright, I stood reverently before him, asking in prayer that I might look at him without sin. 'Go,' he said, 'announce to the Romans that Heaven wishes that my Rome shall be the capital of the earth; therefore they shall cultivate the

military; they shall know and teach their descendants that
no human might can resist Roman arms.' He said this and
went away on high." (Dungan and Cartlidge, 155)

Johnny Come Lately

Though John 20:19–20 clearly presupposes the presence of all
the disciples at the appearance of the resurrected Jesus, John
retroactively excepts Thomas because he wants to use him as a
symbol for his readers, who of course did not see the Risen Jesus
and may feel themselves at a permanent disadvantage. The story
is of a piece with Philostratus' story of how the ascended master
Apollonius satisfied the doubts of a skeptical disciple.

> The young man in question . . . would on no account
> acknowledge the immortality of the soul, and said, "I
> myself, gentlemen, have done nothing now for nine months
> but pray to Apollonius that he would reveal to me the truth
> about the soul; but he is so utterly dead that he will not
> appear to me in response to my entreaties, nor give me any
> reason to consider him immortal." Such were the young
> man's words on that occasion, but on the fifth day follow-
> ing, after discussing the same subject, he fell asleep where
> he was talking with them, and . . . all of a sudden, like one
> possessed, he leaped up, still in a half sleep, streaming with
> perspiration, and cried out, "I believe thee." And when
> those who were present asked him what was the matter;
> "Do you not see," said he, "Apollonius the sage, how that
> he is present with us and is listening to our discussion, and
> is reciting wondrous verses about the soul?" "But where is
> he?" they asked, "for we cannot see him anywhere, although
> we would rather do so than possess all the blessings of
> mankind." And the youth replied, "It would seem that he is
> come to converse with myself alone concerning the tenets
> which I would not believe." (*Life of Apollonius of Tyana* 8:31)

On the Road Again

Does anyone think the story of the two disciples meeting the
unrecognized Christ on the road to Emmaus (Luke 24:13–35)
reads too much like vivid eyewitness testimony to be considered

legend? Then consider the parallel provided by a votive tablet
posted in the healing shrine of the god Asclepius in Epidauros,
Greece, in the fourth century BCE:

> Sostrata, of Pherae, had a false pregnancy. In fear and trem-
> bling she came in a litter and slept here. But she had no
> clear dream [the usual medium for revealing the inspired
> prescription from the god] and started for home again.
> Then, near Curni she dreamt that a man, comely in appear-
> ance, fell in with her and her companions; when he learned
> about their bad luck he bade them set down the litter on
> which they were carrying Sostrata; then he cut open her
> belly, removed an enormous quantity of worms—two full
> basins; then he stitched up her belly and made the woman
> well; then Asclepius revealed his presence and bade her send
> thank-offerings for the cure to Epidauros. (Lefkowitz and
> Fant, 122)

A Fine Kettle of Fish

Luke 5:1–12 and John 21:1–13 offer two versions of the same
original story, the miraculous catch of fish. Scholars debate
whether the story began as a resurrection appearance, as it still
meets us in John, or as a miraculous calling of the disciples, as per
Luke. The problem is especially knotty given that the Johannine
version shares elements with the story of Jesus walking on or
by—the Greek preposition *epi* may be translated either way—the
sea (Mark 6:45–52; Matt 14:22–27; John 6:16–21). Some have
speculated that these, too, were initially resurrection stories, and
that what originally frightened the disciples was not seeing a still-
living Jesus walking on the unbroken surface of the sea but rather
beholding the dead (now risen) Jesus walking *by* the sea. They
were alarmed, not at the mode of his locomotion, but because,
the last they knew, Jesus was dead!

I suspect that it was not originally a resurrection story (though
I still discuss it here, since it appears as such in John). Originally
the story came from the tradition of Pythagoras, son of Apollo.

> At that time he was going from Sybaris to Krotona. At
> the shore, he stood with me fishing with nets; they were
> still hauling the nets weighed down (with fish) from the
> depths. He said he knew the number of fish that they had

hauled in. The men agreed to do what he ordered, if the
number of fish was as he said. He ordered the fish to be
set free, living, after they were counted accurately. What is
more astonishing, in the time they were out of the water
being counted, none of the fish died while he stood there.
He paid them the price of the fish and went to Krotona.
They announced the deed everywhere, having learned his
name from some children. (Iamblichus, *Life of Pythagoras*, 36,
60–61) (Dungan and Cartlidge, 55)

In my judgment we can be sure John has taken over a version of the Pythagoras story (though it may already have been
Christianized before it came into John's hands). Why? Simply
because John's story retains the detail about the exact number of
fish although it is irrelevant to his story. It has been retained from
a version in which it did matter (perhaps because someone felt,
as modern commentators do, that the number must mean something). In the original, the story hinged on the hero's correctly
assessing the number of fish in the nets. That was the miracle in
the Pythagoras version. And the whole thing is done for the sake
of freeing the poor fish: Pythagoreans were strict vegetarians.
Christians were not, so it didn't occur to them to have Jesus free
the fish. Rather the miracle shifted to Jesus providing the catch
when the disciples had hitherto caught nothing. The exact number is irrelevant; we only need to know the nets were too heavy
to drag in (John 21:6). No one on the scene counted them. (Nor
would they have. Can you imagine? "You guys go on and have
breakfast with the resurrected Son of God; I'll just count up these
fish!") But the number survives nonetheless, although the story
about Pythagoras doesn't specify what that number is. John's version goes one better by giving an exact number, and it is a very
special number—special to mathematical philosophers like the
Pythagoreans, anyway. One hundred fifty-three, the number of
fish in John 21:11, "happens" to be what Pythagoreans called a
"triangular number;" in fact the sixteenth triangular number. (1)
153 is the sum of $1+2+3+4+5+6+7+8+9+10+11+12+13+14$
$+15+16+17$. (2) 153 is also what you get if you add as follows: 1
$+(1\times2)+(1\times2\times3)+(1\times2\times3\times4)+(1\times2\times3\times4\times5)$. (3) Finally, add
together the cubes of all the digits in 153 $(1+125+27)$ and you
get 153! (Dr. Crypton, 78)

Seeing Double

Christian apologists often produce the imagined trump card that
the resurrection appearances could not have been hallucinations
since, we are told, groups ranging from two to over five hundred
beheld the resurrected Jesus. I will not dwell on the fact that such
a style of argument presupposes that these defenders of the faith
have performed a resurrection of their own, bringing back as
their opponents the Rationalists of the eighteenth century, those
strange half-skeptics who believed the gospel stories were all historically accurate but non-supernatural in nature. It seems clear
to us now that, in the Easter stories, the visit to the tomb is fully
as fictional as the appearance of angels. Likewise we do not take
for granted that Peter, Mary, and the rest actually saw anything
on some far-off Easter morning. So the question of whether they
saw Jesus himself or an hallucination is moot. But, for the record,
yet another ancient text sheds light on the apologists' claims.
Apologists reasonably argue that a group of people could not see
the very same hallucination unless we posit some type of telepa-
thy. But the fact is that people can share visions in the manner of
a contagious chain reaction. Gershom G. Scholem describes such
visionary fervor connected with the seventeenth-century Jewish
messiah Sabbatai Sevi:

> The people of Smyrna saw miracles and heard prophecies,
> providing the best possible illustration of Renan's remark
> about the infectious character of visions. It is enough for
> one member of a group sharing the same beliefs to claim
> to have seen or heard a supernatural manifestation, and
> the others too will see and hear it. Hardly had the report
> arrived from Aleppo that Elijah had appeared in the Old
> Synagogue there, and Elijah walked the streets of Smyrna.
> Dozens, even hundreds, had seen him. . . . A letter written
> in Constantinople notes apparitions of Elijah "whom many
> have seen." (417, 446)

If I hear you saw Elijah or Jesus, I may see him, too. We will
both have "shared" the same hallucination. But that does not
mean we are claiming to have shared the exact same sights and
sounds, as if we were both watching the same TV screen in separate rooms. I may have "seen" Jesus in a white toga, while you

imagined you saw him in a red robe. Mine may have had black
locks, while yours sported brown hair. It would have depended
on what we expected him to look like. We may have "heard"
him say different things or nothing. How fascinating that early
Christian literature both preserves a scene in which a group of
charismatic widows (ascetic women) have simultaneous visions of
the risen Jesus, and pointedly says they did *not* see the same thing
(Acts of Peter 21):

> Then Peter said to them, "Tell us what you saw." And they
> said, "We saw an old man, who had such a presence as we
> cannot describe to you"; but others said, "We saw a growing
> lad"; and others said, "We saw a boy who gently touched
> our eyes, and so our eyes were opened." . . . So Peter praised
> the Lord, saying, . . . "God is greater than our thoughts, as
> we have learned from the aged widows, how they have seen
> the Lord in a variety of forms." (Hennecke/Schneemelcher,
> 304)

Up, Up, and Away

Of the canonical gospels, only Luke depicts Jesus' ascension into
heaven at the conclusion of his "encore" resurrection appearances. Luke's ascension scene seems so close to Josephus' scene of
Moses' departure that it might be based on it.

> All who accompanied him [Moses] were the senate [the
> seventy elders], and Eleazer the high priest, and Joshua their
> commander. Now as soon as they were come to the moun-
> tain called Abarim . . . he dismissed the senate; and as he
> was going to embrace Eleazer and Joshua, and was still dis-
> coursing with them, a cloud suddenly stood over him and
> he disappeared in a certain valley, although he wrote in the
> holy books that he died, which was done out of fear, lest
> they should venture to say, that because of his extraordinary
> virtue, he went to God. (Josephus, *Antiquities of the Jews*,
> 5.1.48)[15]

But Philo of Alexandria's version of this story is similar enough
to show what category of ancient tales Luke's belongs to.

> when he was about to depart from hence to heaven, to take
> up his abode there, and leaving this mortal life to become

immortal, having been summoned by the Father, who now changed him, having previously been a double being, composed of soul and body, into the nature of a single body, transforming him wholly and entirely into a most sun-like mind . . . For when he was now on the point of being taken away, and was standing at the very starting-place, as it were, that he might fly away and complete his journey to heaven, he was once more inspired and filled with the Holy Spirit, and while still alive he prophesied admirably what should happen to himself after his death, relating, that is, how he had died when he was not as yet dead, and how he was buried without anyone being present so as to know of his tomb, because in fact he was entombed not by mortal hands, but by immortal powers, so that he was not placed in the tomb of his forefathers, having met with particular grace that no man ever saw. (Philo, *Life of Moses* 39)

Though each seems to feel the need to be cagey about it, it is plain enough that both writers believed Moses did not really die but ascended into heaven. This was because no one could locate his body; no one knew where (or if) there was a grave.

Were the Easter stories of the gospels typical of ancient Hellenistic myth and legend? You decide.

Chapter Four

Resurrection Texts in the Gospel of Peter

Arthur J. Dewey

Introductory Remarks

H elmut Koester, Dominic Crossan, and I have argued for an early dating and development of the Gospel of Peter. Crossan's creative reinterpretation of the Gospel of Peter in *The Cross That Spoke* has done a great service in drawing our attention to this non-canonical gospel. In this paper I will use my own formal and redactional work on the Gospel of Peter to discuss the resurrection. I do so primarily because my analysis not only suggests a layer earlier than Crossan's reconstructed *Cross Gospel,* but presents another element of so-called resurrection material.[1]

The Resurrection in the Gospel of Peter

The following are the sections from the Gospel of Peter that deal with the resurrection.

---

1. The work of Schaeffer and Brown basically dismisses the possibility of any question of material in Peter being historically authentic. Brown is much indebted to the research of Schaeffer who argues that Peter is neither completely dependent nor independent of the canonical gospels.

Forum 10,3–4 (1994): 177–96

Exaltation at Death

5 It was midday and darkness covered the whole of Judea. They were confused and anxious for fear the sun had set since he was still alive. <For> it is written that, "The sun must not set upon one who has been executed." [2]And one of them said, "Give him vinegar mixed with something bitter to drink." And they mixed it and gave it to him to drink. [3]And they fulfilled all things and brought to completion the sins on their head. [4]Now many went about with lamps, and, thinking that it was night, they lay down. [5]And the Lord cried out, saying, "My power, <my> power, you have abandoned me." When he said this, he was taken up. [6]And at that moment, the veil of the Jerusalem temple was torn in two.

Epiphany

9 Early, at first light on the sabbath, a crowd came from Jerusalem and the surrounding countryside to see the sealed tomb. [2]But during the night before the Lord's day dawned, while the soldiers were on guard, two by two during each watch, a loud noise came from the sky, [3]and they saw the skies open up and two men come down from there in a burst of light and approach the tomb. [4]The stone that had been pushed against the entrance began to roll by itself and moved away to one side; then the tomb opened up and both young men went inside.

10 Now when these soldiers saw this, they roused the centurion from his sleep, along with the elders. (Remember, they were also there keeping watch.) [2]While they were explaining what they had seen, again they see three men leaving the tomb, two supporting the third, and a cross was following them. [3]The heads of the two reached up to the sky, while the head of the third, whom they led by the hand, reached beyond the skies. [4]And they heard a voice from the skies that said, "Have you preached to those who sleep?" [5]And an answer was heard from the cross: "Yes!"

11 These men then consulted with one another about going and reporting these things to Pilate. [2]While they were still thinking about it, again the skies appeared to open and some sort of human being came down and entered the tomb. [3]When those in the centurion's company saw this,

they rushed out into the night to Pilate, having left the tomb which they were supposed to be guarding.

Empty Tomb

12 Early on the Lord's day, Mary of Magdala, a disciple of the Lord, was fearful on account of the Judeans and, since they were enflamed with rage, she did not perform at the tomb of the Lord what women are accustomed to do for their loved ones who die. [2]Nevertheless, she took her friends with her and went to the tomb where he had been laid. [3]And they were afraid that the Judeans might see them and were saying, "Although on the day he was crucified we could not weep and beat our breasts, we should now perform these rites at his tomb. [4]But who will roll away the stone for us, the one placed at the entrance of the tomb, so that we may enter and sit beside him and do what ought to be done?" [5](remember, it was a huge stone.) "We fear that someone might see us. And if we are unable <to roll the stone away> we should, at least, place at the entrance the memorial we brought for him, and we should weep and beat our breasts until we go home."

13 And they went and found the tomb open. They went up to it, stooped down, and saw a youth sitting there <in> the middle of the tomb; he was handsome and wore a splendid robe. He said to them, [2]"Why have you come? Who are you looking for? Surely not the one who was crucified? He is risen and gone. If you don't believe it, stoop down and take a look at the place where he lay, for he is not there. You see, he is risen and has gone back to the place he was sent from." [3]Then the women fled in fear.

Visionary Fragment?

14 Now it was the last day of Unleavened Bread, and many began to return to their homes since the feast was over. [2]But we, the twelve disciples of the Lord, continued to weep and mourn, and each one, still grieving on account of what had happened, left for his own home. [3]But I, Simon Peter, and Andrew, my brother, took our fishing nets and went away to the sea. And with us was Levi, the son of Alphaeus, whom the Lord . . .

The Earliest Layer of Resurrection Material

Background remarks

The most important result of the recent research is the conclusion that the original stage of the Gospel of Peter is the earliest
passion story in the gospel tradition and contains the seeds of all
subsequent passion narratives. The passion tradition begins not
as a simple historical description but as an imaginative response
to the trauma of Jesus' fate, expressed in the stock form of the
Jewish tale of the righteous one who is unjustly persecuted and
subsequently vindicated.

Both Crossan and I have argued that the earliest layer of
Peter follows the story of the Suffering and Vindication of the
Righteous One. Crossan combines three major narrative sec-
tions (Crucifixion and Deposition: 1:1–2, 2:3b–6:2; Tomb and
Guards: 7:1, 8:1–9:1; Resurrection and Confession: 9:2–10:5;
11:3–7). From my own formal and redactional analysis of Peter
I have argued for a simpler version of the story of the Suffering
Righteous One (2:3c–5:1a, 5:2–6:1, 8:1b).

Reconstruction of Earliest Layer: Suffering and
Vindication of Righteous One

My reconstruction of the earliest layer is as follows:

> 2[3c]And he turned him over to the people on the day before
> the Unleavened Bread, their feast. 3[1]They took the Lord
> and kept pushing him along as they ran; and they would say,
> "Let's drag the son of God along, since we have him in our
> power." [2]And they threw a purple robe around him and sat
> him upon the judgment seat and said, "Judge justly, King of
> Israel." [3]And one of them brought a crown of thorns and set
> it on the head of the Lord. [4]And others standing about were
> spitting in his eyes, and others slapped his face, while oth-
> ers poked him with a rod. Some kept flogging him as they
> said, "Let's pay proper respect to the son of God." 4[1]And
> they brought two criminals and crucified the Lord between
> them. But he himself remained silent, as if in no pain. [2]And
> when they set up the cross, they put an inscription on it,
> "This is the king of Israel." [3]And they piled his clothing in
> front of him; then they divided it among themselves, and
> gambled for it. [4]But one of those criminals reproached them

and said, "We're suffering for the evil that we've done, but this fellow, who has become a savior of humanity, what wrong has he done to you?" ⁵And they got angry at him and ordered that his legs not be broken so he would die in agony. 5¹It was midday and darkness covered the whole of Judea. They were confused. ²And one of them said, "Give him vinegar mixed with something bitter to drink." And they mixed it and gave it to him to drink. ³And they fulfilled all things and brought to completion the sins on their head. ⁴Now many went about with lamps, and, thinking that it was night, they lay down. ⁵And the Lord cried out, saying, "My power, (my) power, you have abandoned me." When he said this, he was taken up. ⁶And at that moment, the veil of the Jerusalem temple was torn in two. 6¹And then they pulled the nails from the Lord's hands and set him on the ground. And the whole earth shook and there was great fear. 8¹All the people were moaning and beating their breasts, and saying "If his death has produced these overwhelming signs, he must have been entirely innocent!"

The story pattern of this tale is exemplified in the Wisdom of Solomon (2–5). The actions and claims of a righteous person provoke his opponents to form a conspiracy against him. This leads to an accusation (Pet 3:2?; 4:2?), trial (1:1), condemnation (2:3), and ordeal (3:1–4; 4:1; 5:2). In some instances this results in his shameful death (5:5). The hero of the story reacts characteristically (4:1), expressing his innocence, frustration or trust in prayer (5:5), while there are also various reactions to his fate by characters in the tale (4:3–5). Either at the brink of death or in death itself the innocent one is rescued (5:5) and vindicated (5:6–6:1). This vindication entails the exaltation (5:5) and acclamation (8:1) of the hero as well as the reaction (8:1) and punishment (5:1, 3–4) of his opponents.

Beyond this basic narrative, at a later time was added a miraculous epiphany story, detailing a divine breakthrough and intensifying the vindication of the righteous sufferer. After an introduction (8:1–9:1), we find a heavenly invasion (9:2–3), the miraculous opening of the tomb (9:4), a supernatural appearance (10:2–3), and reaction by witnesses (11:3). One can also note further additions: an empty tomb story (12:1–13:3) and the probable beginning of a resurrection appearance story (14:1–3).

In this analysis, Simon Peter (7:2; 14:3) appears only at a later
or final stage of the gospel's composition. Such conclusions not
only would move the date of the earliest stage of the Gospel of
Peter to the middle of the first century CE, but would challenge
basic assumptions regarding the historical development of early
Christian literature.

The Mythic Basis

In Pet 5:5 one finds the earliest indication of the vindication of
the Righteous Sufferer.

> [5]And the Lord cried out, saying, "My power, <my> power,
> you have abandoned me." When he said this, he was taken
> up.

While it is usually the case that the protagonist in the tale of the
Suffering Righteous One is delivered at the very brink of death,
there are instances of "post mortem" rescues (cf. Wis 3:2–4; 2
Macc 7). In Pet 5:5b the rescue is combined with exaltation,
which is immediately followed by a demonstration of vindication
(Pet 5:6–6:1).

In sum, this brief narrative of the rescue/vindication of the
Righteous Sufferer must be placed formally within the genre of
a Wisdom Tale. As such, one must say that it is already mythic
language. What may well have come originally out of Passion
Prophecy has now been turned into a larger and more developed
narrative.[2]

Crossan has noted that Pet 5:5b contrasts with the canonical
versions (Mark 15:37b; Luke 23:46b="breathed his last"; Matt
27:50b ="yielded up his spirit"; John 19:30="gave up his spirit").
If Pet 5:5b is the point of rescue and exaltation of the Righteous
Sufferer, then "he was taken up" is not a mere euphemism for
"he died," as in the canonical gospels, but a way of speaking of

---

2. Both Denker and Crossan have noted that one can well argue that
Peter is dependent upon earlier material from the Hebrew Scriptures.
Thus, Pet 1:1 may have found its origin in Ps 2:1; Pet 3:4, Isa 50:6–7,
Zech 12:10; Pet 4:1a, Isa 53:12; Pet 4:1b, Isa 50:7, 53:7; Pet 4:3, Ps
22:18; Pet 5:1, Amos 8:9; Pet 5:2, Ps 69:21; Pet 5:5a, Ps 22:1. It is significant that this "prophetic layer" is found exactly in the material that I
have underscored as the earliest layer of Peter.

the Sufferer's translation into another life. The mythic vocabulary of the Suffering Righteous Tale is at work here. The succeeding Gospel accounts (including the later levels of Peter) continue to build upon the structure of the Tale of the Suffering Righteous One. They fill in the skeletal structure with more and more details, including large blocks of Resurrection and Tomb material.[3] They no longer need the subtle "taking up" of Pet 5:5b.[4]

The Epiphany Layer

Redactional Observations

While 8:1–11:7 appear at first blush to be a self-contained unit, there are more redactional problems than simply observing that 11:1–2 serve as a redactional anticipation (Crossan). We have noted the probable earlier layering of 8:1b, and Pet 10:4–5 also presents a curious problem. These lines appear to come literally out of the blue! 10:2c ("and a cross was following them") would be a redactional insertion preparing for the unusual fragmentary material of 10:4–5. In addition, 11:4 is quite unexpected in relation to 11:3. It would seem to have been added to make sense of what follows in 11:4. Koester has pointed out that 10:1 is likely secondary since is contradicts 11:3 and sets up the basis for the sinfulness of those who would cover up the event (11:6) (Koester, 1980:128 n. 72). In light of this last point, 10:2a ("while they were explaining what they had seen") would be a redactional link with the more original 10:2b. Further, 11:1 is both a redactional seam for 10:5, and 11:2. 11:4–6 would appear to move the story from a visionary account to an attempted exoneration of Pilate. Koester sees this as a secondary motif (129 n. 74). Peter 11:7 would end this secondary concern.

---

3. Luke gives us a clue to the development of the notion of "taken up." In Acts 1:2 this now refers to a specific event, differentiated from the Resurrection. The mythic language becomes more and more historicized.

4. Origen, perhaps, retains this original sense of being vindicated through exaltation in his Commentary on Matthew 140: "He prayed to the Father and was heard, and as soon as he cried out to the Father, he was taken up."

The Epiphany Format

When these later redactional elements are removed we can detect
an earlier epiphany story:

Introduction (8:1a; 8:2b–9:1)

8 [1a]When the scribes and the Pharisees and the priests had
gathered together, (they) [2b]went to Pilate and begged him,
[3]"Give us soldiers so that <we> may guard his tomb for
three [days], in case his disciples come and steal his body and
the people assume that he is risen from the dead and do us
harm." [4]So Pilate gave them the centurion Petronius with
soldiers to guard the tomb. And elders and scholars went
with them to the tomb. [5]And all who were there <with> the
centurion and the soldiers helped roll a large stone against
the entrance to the tomb. [6]And they put seven seals on it.
Then they pitched a tent there and kept watch. 9 [1]Early, at
first light on the sabbath, a crowd came from Jerusalem and
the surrounding countryside to see the sealed tomb.

Epiphany (9:2–3)

[2]But during the night before the Lord's day dawned, while
the soldiers were on guard, two by two during each watch,
a loud noise came from the sky, [3]and they saw the skies
open up and two men come down from there in a burst of
light and approach the tomb.

Miracle (9:4)

[4]The stone that had been pushed against the entrance began
to roll by itself and moved away to one side; then the tomb
opened up and both young men went inside.

Appearance (10:2b, 3)

[2b]Again they see three men leaving the tomb, two supporting the third. [3]The heads of the two reached up to the sky,
while the head of the third, whom they led by the hand,
reached beyond the skies.

Reaction of Witnesses (11:3)

[3]When those in the centurion's company saw this, they
rushed out into the night to Pilate, having left the tomb
which they were supposed to be guarding. And as they were
recounting everything they had seen, they became deeply
disturbed and cried, "Truly, he was a son of God!"

The Language of Epiphany

In the above reconstructed story we can detect language from the Jewish apocalyptic tradition. The opening of the skies, accompanied by a great noise, as well as the appearance of enormous heavenly figures in a burst of light points to apocalyptic. We see similar use of Jewish apocalyptic traditions in the Apocalypse of Adam 65:26–66:8. There three heavenly figures appear, who have surpassing glory. According to MacRae this text may be contemporaneous with or slightly later than Peter (256).

The Historicity of the Epiphany Material

It is difficult to argue for an historical basis for this material. The most compelling argument for its historicity is that this Epiphany is witnessed by people outside the Jesus circle. In Pet 9:3; 10:2b; 11:3 it is "those in the centurion's company" who see the epiphany. They conclude from this that Jesus is a son of God. Such a conclusion would not be an unusual cultural response to a heavenly breakthrough.

However, the nature of the event and the language used to describe it make the question of historicity problematic. The apocalyptic language used throughout this material is inherently transhistorical. We are now in a language world that eludes historical assessment. Moreover, we must also consider the polemical and propagandistic nature of the material. Pet 8:3 may well have been written to counter arguments against the resurrection. At the same time, 8:3 shows signs of the early kerygma. Another concern is that this is the only instance of people other than those in the Jesus circle who witness such an epiphany of the Risen One. Why does this not surface elsewhere in the tradition? Is Mark 15:39 an indication of its submergence in the ongoing tradition? Or, is this an attempt to win over Roman support for the fledgling Jesus movement? (So Crossan.)

The Final Layer of
the Gospel of Peter

Redactional considerations

In my earlier work I have argued that Pet 7:1 seems to have been composed with Pet 7:2–3.

7 Then the Judeans and the elders and the priests perceived
what evil they had done to themselves, and began to beat
their breasts and cry out "Our sins have brought woes upon
us! The judgment and the end of Jerusalem are at hand!"
²But I began weeping with my friends. And quivering with
fear in our hearts, we hid ourselves. After all, we were being
sought by them as criminals and as ones wishing to burn
down the temple. ³As a result of all these things, we fasted
and sat mourning and weeping night and day until the sabbath.

Additionally Pet 14:1–3 would seem to be on the same linguistic
level.

14 Now it was the last day of Unleavened Bread, and many
began to return to their homes since the feast was over.
²But we, the twelve disciples of the Lord, continued to
weep and mourn, and each one, still grieving on account of
what had happened, left for his own home. ³But I, Simon
Peter, and Andrew, my brother, took our fishing nets and
went away to the sea. And with us was Levi, the son of
Alphaeus, whom the Lord . . .

Likewise, 12:1b ("was fearful on account of the Judeans, and
since they were enflamed with rage") and 12:3a ("And they were
afraid that the Judeans might see them and were saying") would
seem to come from the same redactional level. The "fear of the
Judeans," as well as the "weeping and mourning" of the disciples,
would suggest a linkage.[5] There may be a reference to the fall of

---

5. Notice that "weeping and mourning" is found in 7:3 and 14:2.
On the other hand, the women at the tomb "weep and beat their
breasts"(12:3,5). I would suggest that the latter is from a different layer
in the tradition. The empty tomb story in Peter has been redacted by
the final editor (e.g. "fearful on account of the Judeans" (12:1), "they
were afraid the Judeans might see them" (12:3). 12:3–4 may well be a
dramatic growth from the original story. Minus the redactional additions, 12:1–2 may well have been part of the core story (along with
13:1a,3). Already in the source for both Mark and Peter we see three
items: a) introduction of dialogue, b) insertion of angelophany, c) insertion of kerygma. Osiek (102) finds in all of the empty tomb stories the
basic core: Mary Magdalene arrives at the tomb first, finds it empty and
goes away confused.

Jerusalem in 7:1–2. Also, for the first time a self-conscious reference of the community over against the "Judeans" appears. An "us vs. them" mentality has arrived along with concern for the Temple's fate (7:2).

At this later stage in the development of Peter the empty tomb story (Pet 12:1–13:3) is folded into the redactional process. Crossan has argued that the empty tomb story in Peter is dependent upon Mark 16:1–8. His argument rests upon the contention that Mark is responsible for the creation of the empty tomb narrative. While fascinated by Crossan's argument, I am not convinced. Despite his point that Mark 16:7 is so "strange" that it necessitated revisions in the subsequent tradition from the slightest (Matt 28:10) to the greatest (John 20:17), I find it difficult to understand why the final redactor of Peter would have removed a verse that would in fact anticipate 14:3. Furthermore, when one removes final redactional elements from Peter's empty tomb story (12:1b, 12:3a), one is left with a format strikingly like Mark 16:1–8 (minus Mark 16:7). I suggest that either Mark has taken his material from Peter or, more likely, that this story existed independently and was used by both.

The Empty Tomb Material (Pet 12:1–13:3)

What usually has been overlooked in assessing the Empty Tomb material is that both Mark and Peter feature women. Osiek has pointedly asked what purpose such empty tomb stories could serve if, as it is exegetically assumed, women could not serve as legal witnesses (97). She also makes the important point that the proclamation of resurrection does not necessitate an empty tomb narrative (102). For both Paul and Acts the core event seems to be the appearances of the Risen One. The silence of Paul and Acts on the empty tomb narratives cannot, however, in Osiek's opinion, be proof of their secondary nature, since the author of Acts knows that tradition.[6] Rather, their silence indicates that the empty tomb tradition is not foundational to the resurrection

---

6. Paul may not know of the empty tomb material due to the original provenance of that material. The "private" stories of women may not have made it into his ken. On the other hand, they may have been known and rejected due to their source (See Osiek, 103–6).

message. But if this is so, then why does this report of women at the empty tomb persist in the tradition?

This lingering question takes on added import when one considers the traditional role played by women in the burial of the dead. While both men and women lament publicly, women carry the burial tradition along with their own culture-specific customs. Such a special role for women in mourning is often perceived as a threat, since women seem to have a closer acquaintance with the mystery of death, and hence a connection with the unknown and the unclean. Empty Tomb stories may have originated in women's storytelling circles and only some time later been combined with more "public" kerygmatic material.

Osiek objects to the commonplace that women's witness would have no legal basis. This is not certain in Mishnaic law. While women were disqualified from serving as witnesses in cases that necessitated bringing accusations against another individual, women could testify in matters of credibility and give testimony in business matters. We need to consider the androcentric bias in transmitting and reading the empty tomb tradition. While these stories did not get into the main (androcentric) stream as early as the appearance stories, the empty tomb tradition may have been passed over precisely because it included stories involving the witness of women. As Osiek puts it nicely, empty tomb stories

> are not considered as proof of the resurrection, not because faith is based on appearances, but rather the other way around: faith is based on appearances, not the empty tomb, because the empty tomb necessitates reliance on the credibility of women, whereas the abundant male experiences of appearances do not. (105)

Yet the tradition persisted, especially the role of Mary Magdalene. Both Thomas 114 and the fragmentary Gospel of Mary indicate this lingering but persistent element of the tradition.

Historicity of the Empty Tomb Material

I would argue that, despite Crossan's argument, it is not certain that the gospel of Peter has used Mark 16:1–8 as its source. Nor can one say that the reverse is likely. More likely, an earlier version of both the Markan and Petrine empty tomb stories existed, since the empty tomb story in Peter has been redacted by the final editor: e.g., "fearful on account of the Judeans" (12:1), "they were afraid the Judeans might see them" (12:3).

12 Early on the Lord's day, Mary of Magdala, a disciple of the Lord, ²took her friends with her and went to the tomb where he had been laid. ³[And they] were saying, "Although on the day he was crucified we could not weep and beat our breasts, we should now perform these rites at his tomb. ⁴But who will roll away the stone for us, the one placed at the entrance of the tomb, so that we may enter and sit beside him and do what ought to be done?" ⁵(remember, it was a huge stone.) "We fear that someone might see us. And if we are unable <to roll the stone away> we should, at least, place at the entrance the memorial we brought for him, and we should weep and beat our breasts until we go home." 13 And they went and found the tomb open. [They went up to it, stooped down, and saw a young man sitting there <in> the middle of the tomb; he was handsome and wore a splendid robe. He said to them, ²"Why have you come? Who are you looking for? Surely not the one who was crucified? He is risen and gone. If you don't believe it, stoop down and take a look at the place where he lay, for he is not there. You see, he is risen and has gone back to the place he was sent from."] ³Then the women fled in fear.

12:3–4 would be a dramatic growth from the original story. Minus the redactional additions, 12:1–2 is then part of the core story (along with 13:1a–3).

The pre-petrine source probably would have contained three items: a) introduction of dialogue (12:3b–5), b) insertion of angelophany (13:1b–2), c) insertion of kerygma (13:2). Osiek finds in all of the empty tomb stories this basic core: Mary Magdalene arrives at the tomb first, finds it empty and goes away confused.[7]

The inclusion of the empty tomb material in Peter does not prepare for what follows (14:1–3). Already the resurrection has been indicated. Pet 12:1c, 3bc, 5de describes the funereal role of women (in distinction from the burial task of males found in 6:4). In Mark 16:1 there seems to be a contradiction between

---

7. Osiek (102) rightly includes John 20:1–2, 11–18 in this survey of possible early material.

what was done for the body of Jesus in 15:46 and what would be
done in the first verse of chapter 16. The burial of Jesus in Mark
seems to be completed before chapter 16 begins. Yet Mark adds
a supplementary attempt at anointing. I would suggest that since
this is a residue of a report of what women would have done at
the burial of Jesus, it strongly intimates an earlier tradition. Peter
much more clearly expresses the specific cultural role of women
in the mourning ritual. I would also contend that this does not
mean a refinement of Mark but indicates that the two traditions
(male and female) are coming together. Mark may actually be
trying (somewhat unsuccessfully) to smooth over these disparate
elements in the tradition.

Furthermore, as noted above, one must come to grips with the
question of why the empty tomb material surfaces and persists
in the tradition. This material cannot be separated from the presence of women (Mary Magdalene, in particular). Indeed, we must
ask whether an androcentric bias has determined not only the
transmission but also the interpretation of this material. Osiek has
correctly noted that the credibility of women witnesses may well
be undermined by such an androcentric bias.

Historicity of the Empty Tomb Story (Pet 12:1–13:3)

From the above considerations I would argue that at least the
textual elements found in Pet 12:1–2, 13:1a, 3 derive from a very
early tradition. Moreover, I propose that Pet 12:3b–5, a dramatic
development of the original, fills in the cultural picture presup-
posed in the action of Pet 12:1–2, namely, the specific mourning role of women, and thus meets the environmental criterion.
I would also argue that this early story goes against the cultural,
androcentric bias. It is suggestive of the private world of ancient
women. What can be said historically is that we have an early
story of a woman (or women) going to the tomb to mourn the
dead Jesus. She finds the tomb empty and leaves bewildered. This
does not point to the resurrection of Jesus as much as to what
happened to some women after the death of Jesus. The subsequent additions to the story fill out the gaps with dialogue and
angelic epiphany. Such additions are due to the difficulty of the
original story.

Chapter Five

Was Jesus' Resurrection an Historical Event?

A Debate Statement with Commentary

Roy W. Hoover

Introduction

On March 10, 2008, I engaged in a debate at Millsaps College in Jackson, Mississippi with well-known evangelical theologian William Lane Craig. The rules for this debate allowed each of us to present an eighteen-minute opening statement on the question of whether Jesus' resurrection was an historical event. We were also allowed time for rebuttals and a closing statement. The time constraints meant that the opening statement had to be rather concise. Some elements of the opening argument had to be somewhat compressed, while other elements could only be briefly noted, because the limited time did not permit the presentation of supporting evidence. This article begins with the text of my opening statement in that debate. The way we address the issue embedded in the topic of the debate affects both how we understand what early Christians meant when they claimed that

The Fourth R, forthcoming 2009

God raised Jesus from the dead, and whether the claim of those ancient believers is capable of carrying any weight of meaning across the centuries into the modern world. While the limits of the format at Millsaps College left no room to address the latter question it is of considerable interest and importance to many of the heirs of the Christian tradition. Therefore I will address that matter in the commentary section of this article, as well as expand there on the argument of the opening statement.

I. My Opening Statement in the Debate

In his opening statement, Dr. Craig has argued that early Christian claims about the resurrection of Jesus began as a response to a supernatural miracle. In my opening statement, I will argue that early Christian claims about the resurrection of Jesus began as an affirmation of their faith.

The Best Place to Begin

The best place to begin, if one wants to understand what the early Christian affirmation of the resurrection of Jesus was really all about, is with the fact that resurrection was a Jewish idea for some two centuries before it became a Christian idea. The idea of resurrection did not come like a bolt out of the blue to Jesus' followers after his crucifixion. It was already a familiar idea to them.

The first reference to the hope of resurrection in the Hebrew Bible/Christian Old Testament is in the twelfth chapter of the Book of Daniel, which was probably written between 167 and 164 BCE by a devout Jew who was confronted with severe persecution at the hands of Antiochus Epiphanes, the King of Syria during that period. In the midst of that terrifying distress, Daniel had a vision of an angel (10:1–9 and following) who assured him that the people of Israel would be delivered and that "many of those who sleep in the dust of the earth shall awake, some to everlasting life, and some to shame and everlasting contempt" (12:2). Daniel is told that those who like him lead their people to remain faithful to God's law will shine like the stars forever and ever (12:3). What the angel revealed to Daniel encouraged him to believe that even if it may seem expedient to submit to the Syrian King's commands, in the end it will become clear to all that being obedient to God's commands is what really matters.

The first two Books of Maccabees, both probably written early in the first century BCE, tell the story of the persecution reflected in the Book of Daniel in more detail. These Jewish texts tell how the Syrian King issued a decree that banned all Jewish religious observances and threatened to execute any who defied his command. In 2 Maccabees we read the story of a mother and her seven sons who were executed one after the other by the Syrian King because they defied the king's direct command by refusing to violate Jewish religious law. When the second brother had been tortured nearly to death, he said to the king, "... you dismiss us from this present life, but the King of the universe will raise us up to an everlasting renewal of life, because we have died for his laws" (2 Macc 7:9). As he is dying, another brother says to the king, "One cannot but choose to die at the hand of mortals and to cherish the hope God gives of being raised again by him. But for you there will be no resurrection to life" (2 Macc 7:14). This heroic mother and her seven sons refused to disobey God's law even though it cost them their lives, because they believed that in the end God would raise them from the dead and then it would become clear to all that obedience to God's commands is what really matters.

This Jewish hope in the resurrection was not a mere flash-in-the-pan belief. It persisted among devout Jews well past the period in which Jesus lived. For example, following the catastrophic destruction of Jerusalem and its temple in 70 CE during the Jewish-Roman War, a deeply troubled Jewish man who wrote the text we know as 2 Esdras asks God why the Romans have been allowed to win the war and destroy Jerusalem. "My heart failed me," he says, "because I have seen how you have destroyed your people and protected your enemies, and have not shown to anyone how your way may be comprehended" (2 Esdras 3:29b–31). An angel explains that in the not distant future God will raise the dead, sentence the ungodly to the place of punishment, but lead the righteous into "a paradise of delight" (2 Esdras 7:36). In this Jewish text also, written about the same time as the gospels of the

New Testament and two centuries after the Book of Daniel, it is
again affirmed that in the end being faithful to God's law, doing
what is right, maintaining your integrity, is what really matters.

So the idea of resurrection appeared in the history of the
religion of Israel as an affirmation of faith and hope in the face of
disconfirming circumstances, at a time when committing oneself
to live under the rule of God seemed a strategy for losers. There
is good reason to believe that that is how the idea of resurrection was introduced into the story of Jesus also: as an affirmation
of faith and hope in the face of the stark, disconfirming fact of
his crucifixion, when in spite of his confident message about the
Empire of God, Jesus of Nazareth was eliminated by the Empire
of Rome.

The Resurrection of Jesus: An Affirmation of Faith

The best reason for thinking that the early Christian claims about
the resurrection of Jesus began as an affirmation of faith is found
in the evidence provided by Paul in 1 Corinthians 15. The evidence of this text is especially important for several reasons.

First, Paul is the only New Testament writer who claims to
have seen the risen Jesus himself. No gospel author claims this.

Second, Paul's letters are the earliest Christian writings we
have. First Corinthians was probably written in the early 50's CE.
The New Testament Gospels were all written from twenty to
forty years or more later.

Third, Paul begins his argument for the credibility of the
idea of resurrection in this chapter by quoting an early Christian
confession of faith that he had received from those who preceded him in the Jesus movement and that he had passed on to
the Corinthians (15:3–5). This means that it is among the earliest confessions of Christian faith that we have, going back to the
time of Paul's conversion and calling to become the apostle to
the Gentiles, about three years after Jesus' crucifixion, and perhaps
even earlier.

We should look very carefully at how this early confession of
faith is formulated. It furnishes us with some very revealing information about what these early Christians, including Paul himself,
thought they were claiming when they said that God raised Jesus

from the dead. Paul tells the Corinthians, "I delivered to you as of first importance what I also received;" then he quotes the creed:

that Christ died for our sins according to the scriptures,
and that he was buried;
and that he was raised "on the third day" according to the scriptures,
and that he appeared to Cephas, then to the twelve.

In his commentary on 1 Corinthians Professor Richard Hays says, "The confession (of faith) itself consists of four clauses. The first and third are the fundamental faith affirmations, while the second and fourth ... provide *supporting warrants* for the fundamental claims in the other two clauses" (Hays, 255, italics added).

In other words, the two principal statements of this confession are those said to be according to the scriptures; the other two lines—he was buried, he was seen—serve as assurances that what is claimed in the two principal statements is really so. German New Testament scholar Hans Conzelmann agrees: the two clauses "he was buried" and "he was seen" are added as *verifications* of the two fundamental statements—that Jesus died and was raised (Conzelmann, 252).

So then if we ask what this early confession of faith indicates about the origin of the early Christians' claim that God had raised Jesus from the dead, the answer is that their claim originated as an affirmation of faith based on scripture as they interpreted it, which was then verified, they believed, when Peter followed by the twelve and others, including Paul, reported that they had seen the risen lord. In this early confession, the affirmation of Jesus' resurrection precedes the reference to the "appearances" logically in this passage, and that invites us to infer that this affirmation preceded the "appearances" chronologically also.[1] It seems reasonable to conclude that the appearances of the risen Jesus—or, their visions of the risen Jesus—were understood by his followers as a confirmation of their faith, not as the basis of their faith.

---

1. The specification of these phrases as conceptual (or logical) and possibly also chronological I owe to Patterson (219). Patterson's view of the origin of early Christian belief in Jesus' resurrection is in several respects similar to my own.

The Empty Tomb Stories

All this raises an obvious question: If the claim that God raised Jesus from the dead originated as an affirmation of faith, where did the Easter stories about the empty tomb come from? The answer is, I suggest, that **the faith that God raised Jesus from the dead generated the empty tomb stories, the empty tomb stories did not generate that faith**. However counterintuitive that might seem, there is significant evidence in the NT writings themselves that that was indeed the case.

First, there is Paul's own testimony that he has seen the risen Jesus. Paul uses exactly the same language about the appearance of the risen Jesus to him as he does about every other appearance he lists here. The key Greek word here is *ōphthē*, the aorist passive form of the verb *oraō*, which means "to see." The fact that Paul uses the same language about his own vision of the risen Jesus as he does about all of the other appearances in his list strongly implies that he regarded Jesus' appearance to him to be the same kind of phenomenon as theirs.

We should also take note of the fact that neither here nor anywhere else in his letters does Paul mention the story of the empty tomb. It appears that the story of the empty tomb played no role in persuading Paul that God had raised Jesus from the dead. There is no evidence that Paul had ever heard the story the gospels tell about the empty tomb. He never mentions it.

There is more. Consider this: **whereas the gospels themselves treat the crucifixion of Jesus as a public event, they treat his resurrection as a private event**. The crucifixion of Jesus was a public spectacle. If CNN had been up and running at the time, you could have seen a film clip of the crucifixion on the evening news. CSPAN could have telecast the whole grisly thing live. The gospel authors leave no doubt that in telling the story about Jesus' execution, they were writing about something that actually happened in full public view. In the Easter narratives, on the other hand, Jesus appears nowhere in public. The risen Jesus appears only to a few, all of whom either had been his followers or became believers. So the gospel authors themselves indicate by the way they tell the Easter stories that the resurrection of Jesus was not an historical event in the ordinary sense of the term: it was not something open to public observation or verification. It was something that happened in the private experience of some of his followers.

Finally, whereas the stories about Jesus' crucifixion in the gospels are substantially similar, the stories about his resurrection are substantially different. What that indicates is that **there is no common tradition behind them**. Each gospel author was therefore free to compose his own imaginative tale about how it must have been, just as Matthew and Luke did in creating their very different birth stories. There is no common tradition behind those stories either.

Theologian Paul Tillich got all of this right when he wrote, "One could say that in the minds of the . . . writers of the New Testament the Cross is both an event and a symbol and . . . the Resurrection is both a symbol and an event"(Tillich, 2:153). That is, the crucifixion of Jesus was an historical event that became a religious symbol, and the resurrection of Jesus was a religious symbol that came to be spoken about as if it were an historical event. Tillich's point, simply put, is that the crucifixion was first of all an historical event, and the resurrection was first of all a faith event—an affirmation of faith.

The conclusion to be drawn is clear: the earliest and best evidence we have shows that the early Christians' claim that God had raised Jesus from the dead began as an affirmation of their faith.

II. Commentary

The Empty Tomb Stories Appeared Late, not Early

Some readers might find one part of the argument in my opening statement somewhat confusing or problematic: that belief in Jesus' resurrection did not begin with the discovery of the empty tomb by certain women on the Sunday morning following his execution. That Easter story has become so embedded in our minds and seems to fit the gospel narratives so well that any suggestion that things did not really happen that way appears to be contrary to the certifiable testimony of people said to be eyewitnesses of extraordinary events on that Sunday morning. Surely we should take such reliable testimony at face value, many traditional Christians would say (and during the debate Dr. Craig did say). The problem with this common view is that it is based on a naïve reading of the gospel texts, not on a careful, discerning reading. The naïve reader assumes that the Easter stories in the gospels are the earliest accounts of Jesus' resurrection that we have, and that they derive from credible eyewitnesses who truthfully reported the amazing things they saw and heard on that Sunday morning. Neither of these assumptions is true. The Easter stories in the gospels are not the earliest claims about Jesus' resurrection in the New Testament, and they are not based on the testimony of eyewitnesses of the alleged events of that Sunday morning. How could that possibly be true, one may ask. What evidence supports such a seemingly audacious claim?

The first indication that the Easter stories in the gospels are not as early as they appear to be is that Paul seems never to have heard of them. As noted above, Paul's letters are the earliest Christian writings we have, and he is the only New Testament author who claims to have seen the risen Jesus himself. This makes Paul our earliest and best source of information about the claim that God raised Jesus from the dead. Further, he tells us that he spent two weeks as Simon Peter's houseguest in Jerusalem just three years after his conversion and calling (Gal 1:18), probably less than five years after Jesus' death. If the amazing stories about an angel or two loitering in or near Jesus' re-opened and empty tomb early on that Sunday morning were literally true, Peter would surely have known about them. According to the Gospel of John, Peter had visited the empty tomb that morning himself. In 1 Corinthians 15—the longest, most extensively developed argument for the credibility of the idea of resurrection in the New Testament—Paul says that he passed on to the Corinthians what he had received about Jesus' death and resurrection from those who preceded him as believers, but he makes no mention of having received the Easter stories the gospel authors tell. Nowhere in any of his letters does Paul ever mention an empty tomb story. It seems reasonable to infer from this that Peter did not report the empty tomb stories to Paul during the two weeks they were together because Peter had never heard those stories either. In fact, there is no evidence that anyone had heard an empty tomb story until it appeared in the Gospel of Mark about forty years after Jesus' death and twenty or so years after Paul defended his own belief in the resurrection at some length in his first letter to the Corinthians. Did Mark draw on an oral version of the empty tomb story? If so, it was unknown to Paul, and, apparently, it was unknown to Peter also. Clearly, Paul's belief in Jesus' resurrection was not based on the Easter tale of a supernatural miracle on day three following Jesus' crucifixion. The evidence from Paul, then, indicates that the Easter stories in the gospels did not circulate early.

Not Based on Eyewitness Testimony

The second indication that the Easter stories are not early is that the stories themselves provide substantial reasons for concluding that they are not based on eyewitness accounts of things that actually happened on that Sunday morning. The key observation to make here is that, whereas the stories in the gospels about Jesus' crucifixion are substantially similar, the stories about his resurrection are substantially different. All four New Testament gospels place Mary Magdalene at the tomb, but Mark, Matthew, and Luke differ about the number and identities of the other women who went to the tomb with her, and John says that Mary went by herself. The gospels also differ in their representations of the announcing angel or angels at the tomb. In Mark, the women see a white-robed angel sitting in the tomb. According to Matthew, there is a considerable earthquake, after which a dazzlingly bright angel descended from heaven, rolled back the stone and sat on it, while the solders sent by Pilate to guard the tomb pass out from fright. Matthew apparently assumes that when the women arrived they saw the angel still sitting on the stone. (It is noteworthy that Matthew does not report that anyone actually saw Jesus walk out of the tomb after the angel rolled back the stone.[2]) According to Luke, the women see two angels standing near them. According to John, Mary Magdalene sees two angels sitting inside the tomb.

---

2. In the apocryphal Gospel of Peter this gap in Matthew's story is filled. In Peter 9:35–39 we are told that the two soldiers guarding the tomb saw the heavens opened and two men descend in great brightness, and that the stone rolled aside of its own accord. The two heavenly men entered the tomb and soon came out supporting a third man whose head rose above the heavens. Even though they are said to have seen such an astonishing display of divine power in action, the two soldiers are said to have obeyed Pilate's command to tell no one about it!

With so many differences in detail, it is very unlikely that we are reading factual reports of remembered events.

The gospel stories of the "appearances" of the risen Jesus are different in each gospel as well. Mark anticipates such an "appearance," but reports none![3] Matthew reports "appearances" only in Galilee. Luke says they took place only in Jerusalem and its surroundings. In John, Jesus is said to have appeared both in Jerusalem and in Galilee. Further, in Matthew, Jesus speaks his parting words to his disciples on a mountain in Galilee; but in Luke, Jesus bids his disciples farewell and ascends to heaven from the Mount of Olives opposite Jerusalem forty days after his first "appearance" to them shortly before Pentecost. Only excruciating gymnastic exercises in harmonization can turn these different stories into one, consistent factual account.

What Kind of Story?

If the Easter story is not a factual report, what kind of story is it and how can we account for it? The best way to get a handle on these questions is to track the gospel authors' sources. Matthew's and Luke's sources are the easiest to track, since they both made extensive use of Mark and Q, the Synoptic Sayings Source. As noted above, Mark tells an empty tomb story, but says nothing about "appearances" of the risen Jesus. If the "appearance" stories in the other gospels are factual reports, Mark would surely have known about them. Such a sensational tale would not have been kept secret in early Christian circles. So the question arises, if he knew about them, why would he leave them out? Without the confirmation of "appearances," the meaning of an empty tomb would have been unclear. Tomb robbers, or body snatchers, most likely—a speculation that Matthew is concerned to put down (Matt 28:11–15). Mark points his readers forward to a future appearance: perhaps the coming of the Son of Man in power (see Mark 9:1).

In any case, Mark was not a source for Matthew's and Luke's "appearance" stories. Neither was Q: no empty tomb or "appear-

---

3. In the earliest and best manuscripts, the Gospel of Mark ends at 16:8 with no appearances. Later manuscripts of Mark supply longer endings which include appearances.

ance" stories there. So Matthew and Luke were on their own here.
But they were not completely left to their own devices. They may
very well have received essentially what Paul says in 1 Corinthians
15 that he, in turn, had received from those who were followers of
Jesus before him:

> that Christ died according to the scriptures and was buried;
> and that he was raised "on the third day"[4] according to
> the scriptures and that he appeared to Cephas, then to the
> twelve (and others, including, last of all, Paul)

These creedal statements probably furnished Matthew and
Luke with all they needed to complete what they regarded as
Mark's incomplete Easter story. They each wrote a plausible and
appropriate inferential tale, in which they describe how it could
have happened or must have happened, in a way that appealed
to the popular religious imagination of their time, half a century
after Jesus' death.

They did well. Their stories have had a long shelf life; they still
appeal to the popular religious imagination.

Matthew and Luke each made essentially the same move in
writing their stories about Jesus' birth: neither Mark, nor John,
nor Q, nor Thomas has a birth story. But Matthew and Luke were
resourceful authors. They each wrote a plausible story about Jesus'
birth that was consistent with their narrative about Jesus' life and
the meaning it held for them—a fitting introduction to each
author's gospel, just as the "appearance" and "ascension" stories
furnished their narratives with fitting conclusions.

There is an important difference, however, between what Paul
means by the "appearances" he refers to in 1 Corinthians 15 and
what Matthew and Luke depict in their stories. What Paul refers
to are "appearances" of the risen Jesus from heaven, as is said about
Stephen's vision in Acts 7:55–56. Matthew and Luke have literal-
ized and materialized the idea of such "appearances:" they depict a
risen Jesus still on earth. What was for Paul a visionary confirmation of his faith has become in Matthew and Luke a miracle story

---

4. "The third day" is an idiomatic expression, not a literal number. It
appears in Hosea 6:2, where it means "after a short time." Matthew and
Luke, exercising the storyteller's license, have turned the indefinite reference into a definite number: day three.

about a god walking on earth.[5] The popular religious imagination has always preferred to be wowed by a miracle, it seems, than
merely to discern the meaning affirmed in a statement of faith.

Why Did They Believe in Jesus' Resurrection?

Thus far in this discussion we have been concerned with clarify-
ing the question of the origin and nature of the early Christian
claim that Jesus had been resurrected from the dead. We have
made a case for the view that that claim began as an affirmation
of their faith, not with reports of a stunning supernatural act of
God on the Sunday morning following Jesus' crucifixion. That
familiar Easter legend began as a pious fiction, not with eyewitness testimony of an actual historical event. But why did early
Christians make resurrection claims about Jesus at all? What persuaded them to entertain such a seemingly unlikely aftermath
to Jesus' crushing rejection and brutal execution in Jerusalem?
The answer is: for essentially the same reason that some religious
Jews during the Hellenistic period (roughly 200 BCE to 200 CE)
confidently affirmed their expectation that those who faithfully
obeyed God's law, even at the cost of persecution or execution,
would be raised from the dead. Both Jewish and early Christian
belief in the idea of resurrection was rooted in their faith in God.
Both groups believed that God was the Creator and Ruler of the
world. Both believed that ultimately, if not immediately, God's
will would prevail in the realms of nature and of human affairs.
For Jesus' followers, if his death was the end of the story, that
would mean that the God Jesus trusted in had been defeated, or
had been shown to be a figment of their religious imagination.
If Jesus' vision of how human life ought to be lived, under God's
generous and just rule, came to its demise in his execution—it
was just the impossible dream of a peasant prophet—then his
followers might very well have concluded that they had been

---

5. Paul Tillich used this phrase in discussing the implications of the
christology agreed to at the Council of Nicea in 325. "Popular piety
did not want a paradox (Tillich's way of characterizing Nicene christology) but a 'miracle.' It desired an event in analogy with all other events
in time and space, an 'objective' happening in the supernatural sense"
(Tillich, 2:144). The early tomb stories represent an earlier, similar form
of popular piety.

misled about what really counts in human life, about what really has the power to determine both their own and the world's destiny. Evidently, they might have reasoned, that power was not the generosity and justice of God, but human self interest and will to power: human institutions and their defenders, political regimes and economic systems. If these are the powers that really rule human life, then faith in God and hope for the resurrection of the righteous dead must be regarded as delusional.

But Jesus' followers did not draw that conclusion. Why not? Most people in Antiquity were not prepared to abandon the notion that the natural and historical worlds in which they lived were ruled by divine power. They held differing views of the nature of that power, but they assumed that divinity of some kind was responsible for the conditions of their existence and the destiny of human beings. No compelling alternative understanding of the mystery of life was available to the peoples of Antiquity. And so early Christians did not abandon their faith in God as life's creator and ruler. They continued to believe in the God in whom Jesus had trusted and continued to be persuaded that Jesus was not mistaken; rather, his teaching was a compelling affirmation and his life a compelling model of what human life ought to be. And so they affirmed that God had vindicated everything Jesus had stood for by raising him from the dead and appointing him the Son of God in power, as Paul says in Romans 1:3–4. That is, the claim that God raised Jesus from the dead expressed early Christians' confidence that in the days to come, and come soon, Jesus' vision of life in the Empire of God would prevail, not that of his executioners. As the mother of the seven martyred brothers says according to Second Maccabees, if God has the power to create life, God also has the power to restore life (2 Macc 7:20–29). The hope for resurrection did not seem to them to be an unreasonable faith.

Two Discontinuities

At this juncture there are both discontinuities and continuities of understanding between early Christians and modern heirs of the Christian tradition. The discontinuities largely have to do with worldview. The idea of resurrection is embedded in the Bible's ancient worldview, according to which the cosmos was co-extensive with what was visible to the naked eye, with the earth at its center, except that God and the hosts of heaven resided just out of sight beyond the stars in the highest visible heavens. The idea of resurrection could be regarded as credible as long as the worldview in which it was embedded was credible. If that worldview were to lose its credibility, ideas and beliefs dependent on it would lose their credibility also. All of us who have seen photographs taken from the Hubble telescope know that the universe that has become visible to the eye of this modern instrument is vastly different from anything our ancient predecessors had known or imagined, if Galileo or Darwin hadn't already convinced us of this. The risen Jesus did not ascend to the heaven regarded by early Christians and the peoples of Antiquity generally as a real place above the earth, just beyond human sight. There is no such heaven. As Seminar Fellow Gerd Lüdemann once remarked, early Christian affirmations of the resurrection of Jesus lost their literal meaning when the ancient worldview was replaced by the world that came into view through the discoveries of modern science (180). Early Christians believed that the God by whose power Jesus was raised from the dead resided in heaven. That makes the ancient world's concept of God as difficult to maintain in the modern world as its concept of the cosmos. As theologian Gordon Kaufman has said,

> Our modern/postmodern understanding of human evolutionary and ecological embeddedness in the natural order . . . makes it difficult to continue thinking in terms of quasi-traditional notions of God (as essentially, e.g., 'creator' and 'lord' of humanity and the world). . . . It has become clear to me that the metaphors constituting these views require drastic reworking in light of contemporary understandings of the cosmos and of the evolution of life on earth. (xiv)

If one finds Kaufman's observation here and many others like it in his published work perceptive and persuasive, as I do, then one will agree that neither the ancient concept of God nor the idea of resurrection which is dependent on that concept can continue to be credible in the modern world. Those ideas were credible in the ancient world because they were compatible with the knowledge about the world that was current at the time. But those ancient concepts are incompatible with what modern science has enabled us to know about how the world really is. No ancient Christians were asked to believe what they knew was not true. No modern Christians should be asked to do so either. It is pointless to claim that educated moderns have to believe in the supernatural as a matter of blind faith. Actually, as I see it, there is no such thing as blind *faith*. The right name for that idea is superstition. Genuine *faith* has always been a perceptive way of seeing things (which may, of course, include what faithless people are blind to). A perceptive way of seeing things today requires of us the intellectual honesty to acknowledge the discontinuities of understanding between the early Christians and the heirs of the Christian tradition in the modern world.[6]

Two Continuities

If the idea of resurrection has lost its literal meaning, does it follow that it has lost all meaning for moderns? It may seem so, at first glance; but there are certain points of continuity in human experience in both of these conceptually and religiously different historical periods that should be noted before we conclude that the ancient hope in resurrection has no surviving meaning for knowledgeable people in the modern world. In the opening debate statement we noted that the idea of resurrection first appeared in Hellenistic Judaism as faith's response to a bitter experience of the fact that what actually happens in history is often unjust and immoral. Furthermore, the historical experience and fate of a nation seems to have no relation to whether it is more or less just than its neighbors or rivals. Wealth, power, and just plain luck seem to be sovereign in this world. Moral ideals seem not to make much difference. The morally principled lose out, the morally unprincipled prosper. If God really is history's ruling power and if God is just, how could this be? Should one conclude that Israel's faith has proven to be a delusion? Does actual human experience demonstrate that a concern for justice

---

6. The fact that many traditional Christians adhere to a literal belief in the ancient concept of God and of resurrection is an undeniable *sociological* fact; but that is not an intellectually persuasive reason to think that those ideas remain believable. *Such persuasion* can only be accomplished by an intellectually honest *theological argument* that takes full account of all of the relevant evidence.

in society and for moral virtue in an individual count for little or
nothing in the end? A resurrection hope was raised among some
devout Jews as a response to such anguished questions: the evidence of present experience notwithstanding, the quest for justice
and for moral virtue do matter and will ultimately be vindicated.
God will restore the righteous nation and will even raise righteous individuals from the dead, in order ultimately to demonstrate the reality of God's power and justice.

Insofar as a resurrection faith expresses a response to the
question of whether the pursuit of justice is worth the struggle,
whether trying to live responsibly and with integrity is worth the
trouble, the resurrection faith of ancient believers is concerned
with actual human experience that is continuous with our own,
not just with ideas that are dependent upon a no longer credible
ancient worldview. What is true may not prevail, but only what
is true can enable us to distinguish what is genuine from what is
contrived. Justice may not be done, but justice is still the only basis upon which life in a truly human community is possible. Evil
may defeat the good, but only the good can nourish and sustain
a humane way of life. To affirm such things is to affirm what is
continuous with ancient resurrection faith: a faith that believes
in the reality and worth of such virtues and values even in the
face of disconfirming evidence, and even if you are not materially
rewarded for living by such a faith. A resurrection faith has always
stood for the justice and moral virtue that are indispensable if human life is to have any final dignity and meaning.

There is a second element of a resurrection faith that is also
continuous with our experience as moderns: the hope and possibility of personal and societal transformation. Ancient resurrection
faith combines the moral demand for justice with the dream of
the fulfillment of life. It represents a marriage of the moral sense
and the imagination that led them to envision the possibility of
renewing the world, in the hope that a renewed world would be
ruled by a greater measure of justice and moral excellence than
there is in the existing world. In a renewed world there would be
a greater measure of meaning and fulfillment and we ourselves
would be transformed from what we are to what we might be.

In the gospel he preached and in the way he lived and dealt
with others, Jesus of Nazareth offered an inspiring vision of life

that acknowledges only the sovereignty of the good—the reign of God. That gospel and that life proved to be appealing and liberating enough to rise up anew after its herald had been struck down. There is both a nobility and a challenge about that vision that still lifts the human spirit and that can persuade us that a life that has no place for such aspiration is not worth living—an assessment that is close to what Socrates, another martyred moral visionary, is alleged to have made.

I have suggested here that what is at the core of ancient resurrection faith is a call for justice and moral virtue and a yearning for transformation and fulfillment, and that in these significant respects our own experience as moderns is continuous with that of the people who created a resurrection faith that reflected the worldview of their time. The ancient forms of their faith cannot credibly be continued in the modern world, but the underlying meaning they affirmed can be, and that meaning can foster among us a new theology and a new religious language that resonates with our understanding and experience of human life in the modern world.

An Historical Discovery as a Modern Parable

There was a dramatic moment in Ken Burns' PBS special series on "The Corps of Discovery" led by Meriwether Lewis and William Clark in 1804–1806 that can serve as a parable about our own search for the origin and meaning of the early Christian claim that God raised Jesus of Nazareth from the dead.

After months of hard-going, Lewis and a small party from the Corps of Discovery reached the Continental Divide. One of the film's commentators reconstructed the drama of that moment. For more than three hundred years, he said, people in Europe and America had believed that there was a Northwest Passage, a water route by which one could move across the entire North American continent all the way to the Pacific Ocean. President Thomas Jefferson had commissioned Lewis and Clark to try to find that passage. All of the hopes and expectations of three centuries accompanied Lewis and his men as they walked up the long slope that morning, the commentator suggested. As he climbed, Lewis knew that when he reached its crest, he might be able at long last to see what for so long so many had hoped for and had looked for in vain—the Northwest Passage. But when he reached the crest and looked west, what came into view were still more mountains, stretching as far as the eye could see. One of the major hopes of the expedition was thus disappointed. Lewis had to come to terms that morning with the way things really were: there was no Northwest Passage. The geography of the Northwest was very different from what so many had hoped for and dreamed of for so long.

But that morning of disappointment was also a morning of discovery. Lewis found himself looking out on a vast new territory of stunning natural beauty and an invitation to a new period of history with prospects that far exceeded anything even Thomas Jefferson was capable of imagining.

Some who walk up the long slope toward the continental divide of history and faith, hoping to find that historical knowledge will confirm forms of faith transmitted by Christian tradition for centuries, may be disappointed by what they see: there is no Northwest Passage to the Great Ocean. But that disappointment too can be a discovery: a coming into view of a vast new territory of insight and meaning to explore and live in. And that makes it worth the journey.[7]

-----

7. A more extensive discussion of the subject of this article, including an analysis of the ancient Egyptian belief in life after death, can be found in my article, "Realities and Illusions: Resurrection and Life After Death," in *Forum,* New Series 3,2 (Fall, 2002): 277–305. Some elements of this article have been drawn from that earlier *Forum* article. Readers who wish to pursue this topic further will find a valuable discussion in Stephen Patterson, *The God of Jesus,* pp. 211–40.

Chapter Six

The Resurrection, an Obstacle to Faith?

Thomas Sheehan

The Easter victory of Jesus is the bedrock of Christian faith, but it is turned into a stumbling block by the naive and misleading interpretations of the "resurrection" that Fundamentalists are fond of serving up.

Believing in the Easter event in its true scriptural sense is challenge enough for anyone. But when Fundamentalists require that we believe in their fantastical version of the "resurrection," they give scandal in the biblical sense. Far from protecting and preserving Christianity, their pseudo-scholarship distorts the faith, exposes it to ridicule, and finally eviscerates it. Fundamentalism is a form of smiling nihilism, well-intentioned but ultimately destructive.

I wish to offer some suggestions for removing the stumbling block and getting back to the bedrock. Let those who refuse to believe in the Easter victory of Jesus at least understand and reject the real thing and not some farcical version of it.

My suggestions are in the form of brief theses, documented in my book *The First Coming*. On the negative side I argue that the Easter victory of Jesus was not an historical event—it did not take place in space and time—and that the appearances of Jesus

The Fourth R 8,2 (March/April 1995), pp. 3–9

did not require the sighting of a "risen" body in either a physical or a spiritual form.

On the positive side I argue that the Easter victory of Jesus, properly understood from the Bible and believed in by Christians, refers to God's appointment of the crucified Jesus to be the absolute savior of the human race. Christians maintain that this happened outside space and time; it is a matter of faith and not susceptible of proof. Moreover, I argue that the language of "resurrection" is symbolic—it means "awakening"—and that it was not the original, binding way believers expressed Jesus' Easter victory, nor is it the best. Given its symbolic meaning, I put the words "resurrection" and "risen" in quotation marks.

I begin with a time line that provides some approximate dates within the first century of Christianity (or the Common Era: CE). Then I state my theses on the meaning of the "resurrection" and the appearances of Jesus.

Stage One 30 CE

The earliest proclamations of the Easter victory

The virtually unanimous opinion of mainstream scholars of the New Testament is that the earliest language believers used for the Easter victory of Jesus was not "resurrection" but "exaltation" to glory directly from the cross. Nor do the earliest proclamations contain any references to the discovery of an empty tomb or the appearance of angels to women on Easter Sunday morning.

The source tradition or Q, which originates before 50 CE and bears witness to the earliest Christian faith, nowhere mentions Jesus' "resurrection." However, it does proclaim Jesus' exaltation to glory, as do the pre-Pauline hymns recorded in Philippians 2:8–11 and 1 Timothy 3:16. None of these first-century records offers grounds for postulating "resurrection" as the first or even the best way to speak of Jesus' Easter victory. Not only is the language of "resurrection" absent from this earliest tradition; it is neither essential to nor normative for faith in Jesus. When it was eventually employed, the symbol of "resurrection" was at best only one among many ways to proclaim the Easter victory of Jesus.

Philippians Hymn
Phil 2:6–11

Being in the form of a god (or God)
Did not consider it a thing to be grasped
The being equal with a god

But he emptied himself
Taking the form of a slave
Becoming in the likeness of humans

And finding himself in the human scheme,
He humiliated himself
Becoming obedience all the way to death
Even the death by crucifixion.

For this God has super-exalted him
Gracing him with the name
A name superior to all names

So that at Jesus' name
Every knee should bow down
In the heavens, on the earth and in the underworld

And every tongue should shout out,
"The Lord is Jesus the anointed
For the glory of God the father."

*This early hymn is embedded in the Letter of Paul to the
Philippians. It is a good example of an exaltation.*

Translation by Bernard Brandon Scott

Stage Two 50–65 CE

The earliest proclamations of the "resurrection"

The earliest texts that speak of the Easter victory in terms of the
"resurrection" and appearances of Jesus (as contrasted with his
exaltation to glory) were written some twenty to thirty-five years
after the death of Jesus. They appear in the epistles of Paul, com-

posed from around 50 to 65 CE. Just as in the first twenty years of
Christianity (30–50 CE), so too in these earliest Christian writings
we find no narratives of the "resurrection" or the appearances,
that is, no descriptions or detailed stories about Easter Sunday
and the weeks that followed it.

Instead, we have only brief proclamations of faith, bereft
of virtually any details. Alongside the earlier expression (God
"exalted" Jesus), these proclamations generally take two forms:
God "awoke" Jesus from the dead, and "Jesus was made manifest"
to so-and-so. For the first four decades of Christianity, up to the
year 70 CE, those simple affirmations—brief telegraphic statements of faith—are all we have as accounts of the "resurrection"
and appearances.

Some of these Easter-victory proclamations found in Paul's
epistles go back to earlier years and thus offer insights into early
formulations of Christian belief. One such proclamation is 1
Corinthians 15:3–8, which Paul wrote down around 54 or 55 CE
but which goes back at least into the forties and perhaps into the
thirties. The proclamation makes no mention of an empty tomb,
much less of its discovery by women on Easter Sunday morning.
Rather, the two key words in the Greek text are

- *egegertai*: Jesus was "awakened" by God from the dead (or "was
  raised"); and
- *ōphthē*: Jesus "was made manifest" (or "appeared") to certain
  people, including Peter, various disciples, and lastly Paul.

Regarding *egegertai* and "resurrection"

The primary and literal meaning of the verb *egeirō*, from which
egegertai is derived, is "to awaken someone from sleep." For
example, when the disciples, storm-tossed in their boat on the
Sea of Galilee, cry out to the sleeping Jesus for help, the Greek of
Mark's Gospel says they *egeirousin* him (4:38). They do not "resur-
rect" Jesus, they awaken him. (See also Acts 12:7, where an angel
awoke—*egeiren*—Peter in prison.)

This metaphor of awakening someone from sleep—in the case
of Easter, from the eternal sleep of death—underlies most of the

Pauline scriptures about "resurrection," including the earliest one, 1 Thessalonians 1:10. There Paul urges his followers "to wait for God's son from heaven, whom He awoke (*egeiren*) from the dead." But Paul understands the symbolic nature of his language in this text and makes no commitment to the Fundamentalist's preternatural physics of a body shedding graveclothes and exiting from a tomb. The same holds for the use of *egeirō* in the "resurrection" proclamation in 1 Corinthians 15:4: Jesus "was awakened on the third day."

- Regarding "*ophthē*" and "appearances." The verb-form *ophthē* in 1 Corinthians 15:5–8 means that Jesus "was made manifest" to various people or "showed himself " ("appeared") to them. But the text makes no claim that Jesus appeared in a body, be it natural or supernatural, that the disciples might see and touch. Those stories would come thirty years later.

The Septuagint, the Greek version of the Jewish Bible, often uses the same verb-form—*ophthē*—to indicate that God revealed something to someone, but without specifying any kind of physical or visual seeing. In fact, God appeared—*ophthēn*—to Abraham as a voice, not a vision (Exod 6:3 with Gen 21:1).

Paul, who claims to have received an appearance of the risen Jesus (1 Cor 15:8), was blinded and saw no one—he heard only a voice—during his experience on the way to Damascus (Acts 9:4–8; cf. 22:7, 26:14). Later Paul referred to this event not as a visual appearance but as an apocalyptic "revelation" (*di'apokalypseōs*, Gal 1:12). God, he says, "was pleased to reveal his son in me" (Gal 1:16)—this, without any mention of visual or physical details. This revelation/appearance to the blinded Paul could have been, for example, a voice, a mystical experience, or the bestowal of spiritual insight. It certainly was not the physical appearance of a visible body.

In brief: For the first forty years of Christianity—from 30 to 70 CE—the verbs *ophthē* in 1 Corinthians (Jesus "was made manifest") and *apocalypsai* in Galatians (God chose to "reveal" his son in Paul) are basically the only ways the scriptures announce Jesus' appearances, and they in no way entail that the disciples visually sighted a physical or supernatural body.

The same text in 1 Corinthians proclaims that God awoke Jesus from the dead "on the third day" (15:4). In the Bible "the third day" is not a chronological designation and has no specific temporal significance. And here it is certainly not to be confused with "the first day of the week" (Easter Sunday) mentioned in Mark 16:2. Rather, "the third day" is the Bible's way of symbolically indicating any moment in which God acts to save someone from dire straits. Since "the third day" does not mean "three days later," the text from 1 Cor 15:4 does not teach that the "resurrection" took place on the "third day after the crucifixion," that is, on Easter Sunday.

6"Come, let us return to the Lord; for it is he who has torn, and he will heal us; he has struck down, and he will bind us up.
² After two days he will revive us; on the third day he will raise us up, that we may live before him.
—Hosea 6:1–2

Stage Three 70 CE

The earliest story about Easter

For the first four decades of Christianity, the best we have about Easter are brief proclamations of faith in Jesus' victory, accompanied by no historical information about where or when or how this victory took place. Only by 70 CE, in Mark 16:1–8, do we finally get the first story about the events that allegedly occurred on Easter Sunday morning, complete with legends about an empty tomb and an angel's proclamation of Jesus' "resurrection."

However, even this earliest Easter narrative—written forty years after the events it purports to relate—is extremely minimalist in form and content. According to Mark, Jesus does not appear to anyone after his death. Indeed, Mark 16:1–8 indicates that:

- After his burial Jesus is never seen again; and
- The women who discover the empty tomb and hear the angel proclaim the "resurrection" flee the tomb in fear and tell no one about these events.

Thus the earliest narrative about Easter Sunday morning gives hardly any grounds for the traditional story of Easter that Christians are accustomed to hear proclaimed from the pulpit.

Stage Four 85–95 CE

The elaborate narratives of Easter in the later Gospels

Finally, in 85 CE, fifteen years after Mark's very minimalist narrative of Easter, the Gospels of Matthew, Luke, and, a decade after them, the Gospel of John explode with elaborate narratives of events that allegedly took place on Easter Sunday and the weeks following. These imaginative stories first published between fifty-five and sixty-five years after Jesus' death—are replete with detailed accounts of visible, very physical appearances of Jesus.

All of a sudden Jesus has flesh and bones, hands and feet, a body that walks for miles, carries on long conversations, eats parts of at least two dinners, teaches his disciples how to baptize, offers his wounds to be touched, appears and disappears, levitates into heaven, and even (in John's Gospel) offers breakfast to his friends after giving them suggestions on how to fish. These are the stories that Christians usually draw on for their narratives of Easter Sunday.

The explosion of details in these later accounts of Easter includes the following new elements:

- An angel descends from heaven, rolls back the stone from the tomb, and sits on it. (Matthew)
- The dialogue at the tomb between the two angels (no longer just one angel, as in Mark) and the women expands well beyond Mark's account to include a recollection that Jesus had predicted his own "resurrection." (Luke)
- The women (who, according to Mark, told no one) now inform Peter and others about the empty tomb; and Peter visits it (Luke) and, together with the beloved disciple, even sees the burial clothes. (John)
- Mary Magdalene has a private encounter and conversation with the risen Jesus at the tomb site. (John)
- For the first time, elaborately detailed appearances of the "resurrected" Jesus are narrated, and they include Jesus eating food

and allowing his "risen" body to be touched. These appearances happen at various places and times and culminate in:
• Jesus' physical ascension into heaven, which is narrated for the
  very first time around 85 CE, and only in Luke.

Moreover, these differing narratives of Easter in the later
Gospels cannot be harmonized to produce a consistent story,
without doing violence to the accounts both individually and as
an ensemble. The various Easter narratives contradict one another
egregiously on such matters as:

• who went to Jesus' tomb, and when, and why
• how many angels showed up in or around the tomb
• what the angel or angels said to the women
• what the women did after they encountered the angels
• who received the first appearance of Jesus
• how often Jesus appeared to the disciples, and to which disciples, and where, and when
• whether or not Jesus gave the Holy Spirit to them, and if so,
  when
• whether or not he ascended visibly and bodily into heaven
  (only Luke says that he did)
• if Jesus did ascend into heaven, whether he did so on Easter
  Sunday, or forty days later on Ascension Thursday. (Luke provides both dates.)

Reading the Biblical Facts

Over a period of more than six decades—from 30 CE to the end
of the first century—the Christian community's belief in Easter
developed through four stages, from the barest, unembellished
proclamations of Jesus' "exaltation" to glory with no mention of
"resurrection," up to the later Gospels' quite elaborate accounts
of what the risen Jesus did, hour by hour, on the first Easter
Sunday. How does the Fundamentalist exegete interpret this
development?

In the usual procedure, the Fundamentalist takes the four
very different stages of announcing the Easter victory and the
appearances and, violating every rule of serious scholarship, col-

lapses them into one harmonious account of post-crucifixion events running from Easter Sunday, April 9, 30 CE, to Ascension Thursday, May 27, 30 CE.

In this compressed and twisted fabrication, the Fundamentalist uses the later and very elaborate accounts in Matthew, Luke, and John to violently reinterpret the earlier proclamations in Paul's epistles. Flying in the face of both history and scholarly exegesis, the Fundamentalist disregards the different literary forms of these separate accounts, wipes out the years that separate them, and reads the legendary stories of the eighties and nineties back into the utterly minimalist proclamations of the earliest Church.

Thus, whereas Paul proclaims that the appearances of Jesus consisted simply in his being "made manifest" or "revealed" to various witnesses, the Fundamentalist uses Luke's imaginative account of Easter Sunday evening in the upper room (written around 85 CE), or John's accounts (written in the nineties), to restage those appearances, and insists that they necessarily entailed the ocular sighting and physical touching of a "risen" body that walked, talked, ate, and levitated.

And while Paul and the gospels simply proclaim that God "awoke" Jesus from the eternal sleep of death and appointed him the Christ in the final age of salvation, the Fundamentalist rewrites Paul's Easter victory texts and forces them to announce a literal, physical, historical event that happened inside a tomb very early on Easter Sunday morning.

The Fundamentalist claims that Easter consisted of (a) Jesus' returning from the dead in a "real" body albeit a "new" and "spiritual" one, then (b) his quite literally "passing through" the graveclothes in which he had been wrapped, and finally (c) his physical evacuation of the tomb, although "by means other than the doorway." I quote here from one of the best known Fundamentalist apologists of the "resurrection," Professor Gary Habermas (157f).

Of course, anyone is free to believe such ignorant and unbiblical nonsense if they wish, and even to maintain that it represents the true meaning of Jesus' Easter victory. In Fundamentalist doctrine, such fantasies are the norm. However, these reveries find no support among today's mainstream professional exegetes and theologians, men and women who, without sacrificing one iota

of the content of their biblically inspired faith, also refuse to sur-
render one bit of the scholarly gains in exegesis made by their
God-given reason.

Fundamentalists like Professor Habermas seem supinely ignorant of the category mistake they make when they take God's
supernatural, eschatological act—rescuing the crucified Jesus from
death and appointing him the coming Son of Man—and reduce
it to the status of an allegedly historical event in space and time.
If this were done intentionally, we would call it blasphemy. But it
is done in ignorance, and we must be more kind. Still, the conse-
quences of it are no less pernicious.

Informed Christians, who understand the New Testament
rather than just parrot its words, know that the Easter narratives
in the gospels are not literal accounts of historical events that
supposedly took place during the six weeks after the crucifixion.
They also know that the Easter victory did not happen on Easter
Sunday or on any other day in time.

The Easter victory of Jesus was an eschatological occurrence,
beyond space and time—a meta-historical act of God that took
place "in heaven" when the crucified Jesus died on earth. And it
could no more be observed by human beings within history than
could Lucifer's fall from grace or the entrance of one's great-
grandmother into heaven.

The theological meaning of Easter is not that Jesus "came back
to life" in a spiritualized body, passed through graveclothes, and
exited (presumably naked: John 20:6–7) from his tomb. Easter has
nothing to do with angels literally and historically showing up in
an empty tomb (all non-Fundamentalist exegetes agree the angels
are a literary invention of the early Church), and it does not cli-
max in Jesus' physical ascension into heaven.

These are inspiring myths and legends that the gospel writers
used to communicate the extra-historical, supernatural reality of
God's "awakening" of Jesus from the dead and "exalting" him to
heaven. They are not events of or within history, and for an exegete or theologian to claim they are is professionally irresponsible.

The theological content of Easter is that God

• rescued Jesus from the fate of eternal death and
• appointed him to be the absolute savior, the Christ, who

would return at the imminent end of history to usher in the eternal reign of God.

In the symbolic, apocalyptic language of the New Testament, God

- awoke Jesus from the dead, exalting him to God's right hand, and
- designated him the coming Son of Man.

To put this in biblical shorthand, the Easter victory consisted in God's "Christopoetic" or "Christ-making" act. I take the phrase from Acts 2:36, which says in Greek that God made Jesus be the Christ (*Christon epoiēsen*), that is, meta-historically appointed the crucified Jesus to be the coming agent of definitive salvation. The Christian believes God did this not three days after the crucifixion but at the very death of Jesus on the cross.

In Place of a Conclusion

Much more can and should be said about the Easter victory of Jesus, but there is one path not worth taking.

The distinction between the symbolic, apocalyptic language the Bible uses about Easter and the true Christian meaning of that language is the *pons asinorum*, the "bridge of jackasses," that separates naive, backwater interpretations of Easter from professional, mainstream exegesis. To cross that bridge is to leave ignorance behind. Unfortunately, Fundamentalists like Professor Habermas or, for that matter Rev. Jerry Falwell, because they insist on riding Balaam's ass to their Scripture classes, will never get over that bridge.

We have already cited Habermas, but Falwell is equally clear on how the Fundamentalist approaches the biblical accounts of Easter: "The Bible is absolutely infallible, without error in all matters pertaining to faith and practice, as well as in areas such as geography, science, history, etc." (1980:63).

This a priori commitment to the total inerrancy and literal truth of the Bible is the Fundamentalist's cheap and easy ticket to escape the hard exegetical work that the Christian scriptures require. Preachers like Habermas and Falwell, despite their academic pretensions, opt for the revivalist's tent rather than the scholar's study. They exclude themselves from the circle of professional Christian exegetes and exile themselves to the self-imposed ghetto of unscholarly literalism.

That is their choice. But let it not be called Christian scholarship. Christianity is not defended by fudging the facts, nor is it advanced by sleight-of-hand exegesis. And God is not served by telling lies on his behalf.

Chapter Seven

How Did Easter Originally Happen?

An Hypothesis

Thomas Sheehan

C hristian piety holds that Jesus' existence on earth extended beyond his death on Good Friday and spilled over into a miraculous six-week period that stretched from his physical emergence from the tomb on Easter Sunday morning, allegedly on April 9, 30 CE, to his bodily ascension into heaven forty days later, on Thursday, May 18, 30 CE.

To judge from the Gospels, it would seem that the activities of the risen Jesus during the forty days after he died included: one breakfast; parts of two dinners; one brief meeting in a cemetery; two walks through the countryside; at least seven conversations (including two separate instructions on how to forgive sins and baptize converts)—all of this climaxing in his physical ascension into heaven from a small hill just outside Jerusalem. Impossible though the task is, if we were to try to synthesize the gospel stories into a consistent chronology of what Jesus did during those hectic six weeks between his resurrection from the dead

The Fourth R 14,4 (July/August 2001), pp. 3–8

and his ascension into heaven, the agenda would look something like the following chart. It is clear that the scriptural stories about this six-week period contradict one another with regard to the number and places of events, and even the date and the loca-

---

Chronology of Jesus' Alleged Easter Activities
Sunday, April 9, 30 CE
The Jerusalem Area

Morning

1. Jesus rises from the dead early in the morning (Mark 16:9). Mary Magdalene, alone or with other women, discovers the open tomb. Either she informs Peter and another disciple, who visit the tomb and find it empty (John 20:1–10); or she and the others meet one or two angels inside, who announce the resurrection (Mark 16:5–6; Luke 24:4–6); or the women flee and say nothing to anyone (Mark 16:8).

2. Later, outside the tomb, Jesus appears to Mary Magdalene alone, who at first mistakes him for a gardener. He tells her to inform the disciples that he is ascending at that moment to his Father (John 20:17; Mark 16:9).

3. Jesus also appears to Mary Magdalene and another Mary, who grasp his feet and worship him. Jesus tells them to send the brethren to Galilee, where they will see him (Matt 28:10).

Afternoon and early evening

4. Sometime during the day Jesus appears to Simon Peter (Luke 24:34).

5. Jesus walks incognito through the countryside for almost seven miles with two disciples. He starts to eat dinner with them in Emmaus but disappears as soon as they recognize who he is (Luke 24:13–31; Mark 16:12–13).

Evening

6. Back in Jerusalem, Jesus appears to the disciples in a room even though the doors are locked. He tries to overcome their doubts by showing them his wounds and by eating broiled fish and honeycomb. He either gives them the Holy Spirit and the power to forgive sins (John) or does not (Luke), and either sends them out into the whole world (Mark) or tells them to stay in Jerusalem for a while (Luke). The disciple Thomas either is present (Luke

and Mark, by implication) or is not (John) (Luke 24:36–49; John 20:19–23; Mark 16:14–18).

7. Jesus ascends into heaven that night from Bethany (Luke 24:51; Mark 16:19).

Sunday, April 16, 30 CE
Still in Jerusalem

8. Jesus appears again to the disciples behind locked doors, and invites Thomas, who now is present, to put his fingers and hands into the wounds (John 20:26–29).

Over the next weeks

9. Jesus offers the disciples many other proofs and signs, not all of which are recorded in the Gospels (John 20:30).

Late April or early May, 30 CE
Galilee

10. Early one morning Jesus makes his "third appearance" (sic, John 21:14), this time to Simon and six others on the shore of Lake Galilee. He miraculously arranges for them to catch 153 large fish and invites them ashore for a breakfast of broiled fish and bread, which he has prepared. Jesus instructs Simon, "Feed my lambs, feed my sheep," and discusses how Simon and the Beloved Disciple will die (John 21:1–23).

11. Jesus appears to the eleven disciples on a mountain, but some still doubt. He commissions them to baptize all nations and assures them, "I am with you always, to the close of the age." He does not ascend into heaven (Matt 28:16–20).

Thursday, May 18, 30 CE
Back in the Jerusalem area

12. Jesus appears again and tells the disciples to wait in Jerusalem until they receive the Holy Spirit (even though, according to John, they had already received the Spirit on April 9: John 20:22). Then he ascends into heaven from Mount Olivet, just west of Jerusalem (Acts 1:1–12).

Sunday, May 28, 30 CE

13. God sends the Holy Spirit upon the twelve disciples, Mary, the mother of Jesus, and about 107 other people (Acts 2:1–4; cf. 1:13–15, 26).

tion of the ascension into heaven. Despite one's best efforts, the gospel accounts of Jesus' post mortem activities in fact cannot be harmonized into a consistent "Easter chronology." Nor need we bother to ask if the miraculous events of this Easter period could have been observed or recorded by cameras or tape recorders, had such devices been available. The reasons both for the patent inconsistencies and the physical unrecordability of these miraculous "events" come down to one thing: The gospel stories about Easter are not historical accounts but religious myths.

In any case, the New Testament does not in fact assert that Jesus came back to life on earth, or that he physically left his grave alive after he had died, nor does it maintain that faith in him is based on an empty tomb. What is more, almost forty years would pass after Jesus' death before the Christian Scriptures so much as mentioned an empty tomb (Mark 16:6, written around 70 CE), and it would take yet another ten to twenty years after that (ca. 80–90 CE) before the Gospels of Matthew and Luke would claim that Jesus' followers had seen and touched his risen body.

If Christianity stands or falls with the resurrection, may we ask when Jesus was raised from the dead? The Scriptures make no attempt actually to date the resurrection to Easter Sunday morning, nor do they claim that anyone saw Jesus rise physically from the dead and exit the tomb. They do not even assert that the resurrection took place at Jesus' tomb. In fact, catechetical popularizations aside, Christianity does not claim that the resurrection was an historical event, a happening in space and time.

But if the gospel accounts of Easter are myths rather than historical accounts, what actually did happen after the crucifixion? Bereft as we are of historical access to the resurrection, we find ourselves thrown back on the claims of Simon Peter and other early believers that they had certain religious experiences ("appearances") which convinced them that Jesus continued to exercise power after his death. The first recorded claim of such appearances (1 Cor 15:5–8) was not written down until Paul did so some twenty-five years after the crucifixion.

Let us attempt to imagine a scenario of historical events that actually took place in the days and weeks after Jesus died.

Reconstructing the Original Easter

According to the best scholarly estimates, the last historical event in the life of Jesus of Nazareth was his death on April 7, 30 CE, following the torture of crucifixion. No coroner was present to record the medical facts, but the Scriptures and the Christian creed put the matter simply and directly: He died and was buried. Jesus had not fainted. He was dead. And in the spirit of the New Testament we may add one further datum: He never came back to life.

The Passover festival of 30 CE came and went, and life returned to normal. Jesus' closest disciples probably knew of his death only by hearsay. Most likely they had not been present at the crucifixion and did not know where he was buried. Having abandoned Jesus when he was arrested, they had fled in fear and disgrace to their homes in Galilee. There, grieving at their loss, they faced the crushing scandal of those last days in Jerusalem.

The scandal was not that Jesus had been condemned to die on the cross. Traumatic as it was for the disciples, the murder of Jesus was not entirely a surprise; indeed, it seemed to be almost inevitable. Death was the price that heroes like him had long paid (John the Baptist was only the most recent case) for threatening the cherished world of the religious establishment and the vaunted omnipotence of empire. Jesus had known what was in store for him, and had accepted it with courage, trusting himself without reserve to the cause of God with humankind. By living the kingdom and becoming what he lived, Jesus demonstrated his conviction that not even his death could cancel God's presence. This is what Jesus finally meant by "Abba": everything, even death, was in the hands of his loving Father.

The scandal of those last days in Jerusalem was not that Jesus was crucified, but that the disciples lost faith in what he had proclaimed. Jesus' every word had been a promise of life, but the disciples fled when threatened with death. He had trusted utterly in God; but they feared other men. On the night before Passover, they abandoned Jesus to his enemies, just after sharing with him the cup of a fellowship that was supposed to be stronger than death.

We can imagine the scene. Simon, later to be called Cephas or Peter—a fisherman perhaps thirty years of age—has returned in haste to Capernaum, his village on the Sea of Galilee. He thinks of his friend, whose body has begun to rot in a grave outside Jerusalem. Long after the event Matthew reconstructs Peter's thinking. He has him recall their last meal together.

> Simon declared to Jesus, "Though they all fall away because of you, I will never fall away!" Jesus said to him, "Truly, I say to you, this very night, before the cock crows, you will deny me three times." Simon said to him: "Even if I must die with you, I will not deny you."
>
> —Matt 26:33–35

Matthew has Simon remember the darkness of Gethsemane that same night as Jesus went ahead into the grove to pray. Suddenly the arrival of armed men, the torchlight red on sweaty faces, a kiss of betrayal. Then Simon's cowardly flight through the olive grove and away into the night.

A Key Role for Simon in the Construction of Easter

Throughout the gospels and in the early part of Acts, Simon is a central character. So let us imagine a role for Peter that was so special that it could give rise to these later traditions.

In those dark days after Jesus' death, Simon had a religious insight, a "revelatory experience" that he took as a message from God's future. We cannot know exactly how the insight dawned on him. But we do know that pious Jews of the time felt at home with a broad spectrum of ecstatic visions and manifestations: theophanies (Acts 7:55), angelophanies (Luke 1:11), revelations (Gal 1:12), epiphanies of returning prophets (Mark 8:28), and stories about how Gentiles had converted to Judaism after having visions of blinding light (the way Saul of Tarsus would turn to the Jesus movement: cf. Acts 9:3). It was this lexicon of revelation-experiences that later tradition has Simon spontaneously draw upon when he first tries to put into words the "Easter experience" that he underwent in Capernaum. In his darkest despair, the Father's forgiveness, that gift that was God himself,

had swept him up again and undone his doubts. Simon "saw"—
God revealed it to him in an ecstatic vision—that the Father had
taken Jesus into the God's own power and would send him again
soon, in glory, to usher in God's kingdom.

And having "turned again" under the power of God's grace,
Simon took the lead (Luke 22:32). He hastened to gather Jesus'
closest followers together at his own house and share his experience with them. They all reflected on what they had earnestly
hoped for and renewed their faith. They spoke of their master,
recalled his extraordinary message, and prayed his comforting
eschatological words in a new and fresh way: "Abba, thy kingdom
come!"

They began to call their new leader "Simon Kepha," the rock
of faith. They clung to that rock, and they too sensed the gift of
God's future overcoming their lack of faith. They too "saw" God's
revelation and had their own Easter experience.

There in Capernaum—without having laid eyes on Jesus since
the moment he was dragged off to his trial, without seeing Jesus'
tomb in Jerusalem or hearing that it was supposedly empty—
Simon and the other disciples experienced Easter. We cannot
know the psychological genesis of that experience, but we do
know its result. They believed that Jesus had been swept up into
God's power and would soon return. God's reign would quickly
be realized.

The Jesus movement was born—or rather, was reborn, since
it had already existed during Jesus' lifetime—as Simon and the
others began proclaiming the message of Jesus in the same synagogues of Capernaum, Chorazin, and Bethsaida where he himself
had preached it. "Repent!" they exhorted the people. "The kingdom of God is at hand!"

How did Simon (and the other disciples) put this experience into words? We should not conclude too hastily that Simon
proclaimed that Jesus had been physically raised from the dead.
The "resurrection" was not an historical event but only one of
many possible ways in which Simon could interpret the divine
vindication of Jesus that he claimed to have experienced. In
fact, "resurrection" was probably not the first term that he used
to express what he had "seen." Probably the earliest way that
Simon put into words his renewed faith in God's kingdom was

to say that God had "glorified" his servant (Acts 3:13), that he
had "exalted" him to his right hand (2:33), that he had assumed
him into heaven and "designated" him the agent of the coming
eschaton (3:20)—without any mention of a physical resurrection.
Later believers would say merely that Jesus had "entered heaven"
and "appeared before God." Simon and the disciples probably
used these and other ways to express their Easter experience,
their discovery that Jesus had been rescued from death and been
appointed God's special eschatological deputy.

Of course, the language of resurrection was also available,
but in the apocalyptic context of the times a resurrection did
not necessarily mean that a dead person came back to life and
physically left his grave. Some rabbis, to be sure, did promise a
dramatically physical resurrection at the end of time, when bodies would return with the same physique that they formerly
had (including blemishes) and even with the same clothes. But
these fanciful hopes were only one part of the broad spectrum of
eschatological hopes, which included as well the promise of res-
urrections that entailed no vacating of the grave.

The Gospels, for example, say that Herod Antipas thought
Jesus was really John the Baptist raised from the dead (cf. Mark
6:16). Today we might suggest that the tetrarch could have allayed
his fears by making a trip to the Dead Sea and having John the
Baptist's body exhumed. But that thought probably did not even
occur to Herod (nor to the writers of the gospels) any more than
it occurred to Simon to go down to Jerusalem from Galilee to
check whether Jesus' bones were still in the tomb. In first-century
Palestine, belief in a resurrection did not depend on cemetery
records and could not be shaken by exhumations or autopsies.
Resurrection was an imaginative, apocalyptic way of saying that
God saved the faithful person as a whole, however that wholeness
be defined (see, for example, I Cor 15:35ff.). Resurrection did
not mean having one's molecules reassembled and then exiting
from a tomb.

Regardless of whether Simon used the apocalyptic language of
exaltation or of resurrection to express his identification of Jesus
with God's coming kingdom, neither of these symbolic terms
committed Simon to believing that Jesus went on existing or
appearing on earth after his death. Affirmations of resurrection

or even appearances are not statements about the post mortem history of Jesus but religious interpretations of Simon's Easter experience. And for Christianity, Simon's experience is the first relevant historical event after the death and burial of Jesus.

In other words, according to the popular and mythical Easter chronologies that some Christians try to establish from the Gospels, the order of events after the crucifixion is as follows:

Easter Event	Post-Easter Events	
The Resurrection ➡	The Appearance ➡	The Result
Jesus is raised	Jesus appears to Simon	Simon's faith in Jesus
(April 9, 30 CE)	*(later that day)*	*(soon thereafter)*

However, the actual sequence of events after the death of Jesus seems to be quite different, and on our hypothesis would look like the following.

The Easter Experience	One Formulation of that Experience
Simon, in what he took to be a revelation or appearance, "saw" that God had 1. taken Jesus into the coming future and 2. appointed him the Son of Man. ➡	"God raised Jesus from the dead."

The Easter Experience

I have suggested that something happened to Simon and the other disciples in the order of space and time, perhaps even over a period of time—an experience that could have been as dramatic as an ecstatic vision, or as ordinary as reflecting on the meaning of Jesus' life and death. In any case it was an experience to which no one else, whether believer or nonbeliever, could have direct, unmediated access. In fact, not even Simon could claim unmediated access to the experience he underwent: He knew it only by interpreting it. Eventually Simon and the others who interpreted his role would speak of his experience in one of the many apocalyptic symbols that were at hand: "Jesus has appeared to Simon." But such an appearance need not have been a physical-ocular manifestation of Jesus. Simon understood his experience as an eschatological revelation that Jesus had been appointed the coming Son of Man. Simon now believed that God had taken Jesus into the eschatological future and would send him to usher in the kingdom at the imminent end of time.

A Secondary Formulation of the Easter Experience

The rescue of Jesus from death and his exaltation and imminent return soon came to be codified in yet another of the available apocalyptic formulae: "God has raised Jesus from the dead." Eventually the term "resurrection" became the dominant and even normative word for expressing what Simon and the disciples believed had happened to Jesus.

But even then, for the early believers to speak of the resurrection of Jesus from the dead did not mean that they looked back to a historical event that supposedly happened on Sunday, April 9, 30 CE. The "event" of the resurrection is like the "event" of creation: No human being was present, no one could or did see it, because neither "event" ever happened. Both creation and the resurrection are not events but interpretations of what some people take to be divine actions toward the world. Thus, all attempts to "prove the resurrection" by adducing physical appearances or the emptiness of a tomb entirely miss the point. They confuse an apocalyptic symbol with the meaning it is trying to express.

For Simon and the others, "resurrection" was simply one way of articulating their conviction that God had vindicated Jesus and was coming soon to dwell among this people. And this interpretation would have held true for the early believers even if an exhumation of Jesus' grave had discovered his rotting flesh and bones.

In short, the grounds for Simon's Easter faith were neither the discovery of an empty tomb (Simon most likely did not know where the prophet was buried) nor the physical sighting of Jesus' risen body (this is not what an eschatological appearance is about). Easter happened when Simon had what he thought was an eschatological revelation, which overrode his doubts and led him to identify Jesus with the one who soon would come to bring in God's reign.

Works Consulted

Brown, Raymond E. "The Gospel of Peter and Canonical Priority."
    New Testament Studies 33 (1987): 321–43.
_____. *The Death of the Messiah.* Vol. 2. Garden City, NY: Doubleday,
    1993.
Conzelmann, Hans. *1 Corinthians.* Hermeneia. Philadelphia: Fortress
    Press, 1975.
Crossan, John Dominic. *The Cross That Spoke: The Origins of the Passion
    and Resurrection Narratives.* San Francisco: Harper & Row, 1988.
Dr. Crypton (Paul Hoffmann). "Mathematics in the Bible." *Science Digest*
    (May 1985): 78–79, 91.
Denker, Jurgen. *Die theologiegeschichtliche Stellung des Petrusevangeliums.*
    Bern: P. Lang, 1975.
Dewey, Arthur. "'Time to Murder and Create': Visions and Revisions in
    the Gospel of Peter." *The Apocryphal Jesus and Christian Origins.* Ed.
    Ron Cameron. *Semeia* 49 (1990): 101–27.
Diodorus of Sicily. *Library of History.* Trans. C. H. Oldfather, Loeb
    Classical Library. Harvard University Press, 1935. [Translation slight-
    ly modified by author.]
Diogenes Laertius. *Lives of Eminent Philosophers.* Rev. ed. Trans. R. D.
    Hicks. Loeb Classical Library. Harvard University Press, 1931.
Dionysus of Halicarnassus. *Roman Antiquities.* Trans. Earnest Cary. Loeb
    Classical Library. Harvard University Press, 1937.
Dungan, David L. and David R. Cartlidge. *Sourcebook of Texts for the
    Comparative Study of the Gospels.* Missoula, MT: Scholars Press, 1974.
Falwell, Jerry. *Listen America.* Doubleday, 1980.
Habermas, Gary. *The Resurrection of Jesus.* Grand Rapids, MI: Baker,
    1980.
Hays, Richard B. *First Corinthians. Interpretation.* A Bible Commentary
    for Teaching and Preaching. Louisville, KY: John Knox Press, 1997.

Hennecke, Edgar and Wilhelm Schneemelcher, eds. *New Testament Apocrypha*. Vol. 2. Philadelphia: Westminster Press, 1965.

Josephus. *Antiquities of the Jews*. In *The Works of Flavius Josephus*. Trans. William Whiston. London: Ward, Lock & Co., Limited, nd.

Kaufman, Gordon D. *An Essay on Theological Method.* . Third ed. Atlanta, GA: Scholars Press, 1995.

Koester, Helmut. "Apocryphal and Canonical Gospels," *Harvard Theological Review* 73 (1980): 105-30.

Lefkowtiz, Mary R. and Maureen B. Fant, eds. *Women's Life in Greece and Rome*. Baltimore: John Hopkins University Press, 1982.

Lüdemann, Gerd. *The Resurrection of Jesus: History, Experience, Theology*. Minneapolis, MN: Fortress Press, 1994.

MacRae, George W. "The Apocalypse of Adam, Introduction and Translation." Pp. 256–64 in *The Nag Hammadi Library*. Ed. Marvin Meyer. New York: Harper & Row, 1977.

Miller, Robert J., ed. *The Complete Gospels.* Sonoma, CA: Polebridge, 1992.

Osiek, Carolyn. "The Women at the Tomb: What Are They Doing There?" *Ex Auditu* 9 (1993): 97-107.

Patterson, Stephen. *The God of Jesus: The Historical Jesus and the Search for Meaning*. Harrisburg, PA: Trinity Press International, 1998.

Philo. *Life of Moses*. Trans. C.D. Yonge. In Nahum N. Glatzer, ed. *The Essential Philo*. New York: Schocken Books, 1971.

Philostratus, Life of Apollonius of Tyana. Trans. F.C. Conybeare. Loeb Classical Library. Harvard University Press, 1950.

Plutarch. "Romulus." *The Lives of the Noble Grecians and Romans*. Trans. John Dryden. Rev. Arthur Hugh Clough. New York: Modern Library, c1979.

Segal, Alan. *Life after Death: A History of Afterlife in Western Religion*. New York: Doubleday, 2004.

Sheehan, Thomas. *The First Coming: How the Kingdom of God Became Christianity*. New York: Random House, 1986.

Schaeffer, Susan. "The Gospel of Peter, The Canonical Gospels, and Oral Tradition." Ph.D. Dissertation, Union Theological Seminary, 1991.

Scholem, Gershom. *Sabbatai Sevi, the Mystical Messiah*. Princeton University Press, 1973.

Tillich, Paul. *Existence and the Christ. Systematic Theology*. Vol 2. Chicago: University of Chicago Press, 1957.

Discussion Questions

Chapter 1
Robert W. Funk, *The Resurrection of Jesus: Reports and Stories*
I have developed a large number of discussion questions for this first essay because it deals with a great number of texts. These questions are designed to help you ask the appropriate critical questions about these texts so as to come to terms with an understanding of how early Christians developed an understanding of the resurrection of Jesus.

If you are using these questions as part of a discussion group, you might want to divide these texts over a number of sessions. I have divided the questions into four units or sessions.

Unit I
1. Funk lists three kinds of resurrection texts: lists, reports and stories. Give an example of each type. Can you clearly distinguish between them?
2. What does Funk mean when he says that the resurrection of Jesus is not directly narrated or reported in the New Testament? Why do you think the resurrection is not directly reported? What is the difference between narrating an event and announcing an event?
3. What is the earliest reference to the resurrection in the New Testament? What type is it? A list, report or story? What is the significance of the type? How early is the earliest report of the resurrection?
4. Since Paul lists himself in the list of those to whom the resurrected Jesus has appeared, what does this tell us about resurrection appearances in the pre-70 period?

5. What is the earliest story in the New Testament of Jesus appearing to someone? In what Gospel is it? What is its date? To whom does Jesus appear?

6. What is the significance of Paul putting himself in the list of those to whom the resurrected Jesus has appeared?

7. What is the difference between resuscitation and resurrection? How important is this difference? What does Paul think of physical resurrection?

Unit II

8. What is the earliest narrative allusion to the resurrection of Jesus? In what Gospel does it appear? Does Paul contain any reference to the empty tomb? Of appearances to women?

9. Does Mark ever present an appearance of the resurrected Jesus? How does his gospel end?

10. Matthew follows Mark but then adds what Funk calls legendary material. Why is the material legendary? What makes it legendary?

11. Matthew has Jesus appear and say to the women what in Mark the young man says to the women. Funk says this is an angelophany changing into a Christophany. What does he mean by this?

12. Does Matthew contain any independent material about the resurrection? That is, what comes from Mark, what comes from Matthew and what might come from the tradition?

13. Mark does not have the women report to the eleven (apostles), but both Matthew and Luke do. Why would they do this? Do you think they are reporting what actually happened or do Matthew and Luke have theological reasons for changing Mark?

14. The Lukan story of the two disciples on the road to Emmaus has no parallel in any other gospel. What does this indicate to you about its historicity? What is the significance of Jesus being recognized in the breaking of the bread?

15. Luke knows of an appearance to Peter, as does Paul and apparently Mark, but he does not narrate such an appearance. What might be the significance of this?

16. Luke's story of the appearance to the eleven does not take place on the mountain as in Matthew, nor in Galilee as

promised in Mark. Where does it take place? Why do you
think that this story takes pains to make it clear that the Jesus
who is appearing is not a ghost? That it has flesh and bones?
How does this fit with Paul? What conclusions can you draw
about how resurrection appearance stories are being narrated
at the end of the first century?

17. From where does Matthew have Jesus ascend? From where does
Luke have Jesus ascend? What do you make of this difference?

18. Make a list of the differences between the ascension account
at the end of Luke's gospel and the account at the beginning
of Acts. If these are both from the same author, how do you
account for the differences?

Unit III

19. Why does Funk argue that in the Fourth Gospel the story of
Peter and the other disciple coming to the tomb interrupts
the story of Mary Magdala. Do you find his argument convincing? If so, what does this tell you about the tradition the
Fourth Gospel inherited? Mary does not appear in Paul's list
(no women by name appear in that list) but she does appear
in Mark (Matthew and Luke who are probably following
Mark) and John. What does this indicate to you about the
place of women in the tradition of the resurrection of Jesus?

20. Why does Funk say it is difficult to reconcile the report of
an appearance to Mary Magada in the Fourth Gospel with
Paul's report of the first appearance to Peter? Mark and
Matthew as well as John have the first appearance to woman
or a women, while Paul, the earliest report, has the first
appearance to Cephas (Peter). What is the significance of this?

21. What characteristics of the Thomas story in the Fourth
Gospel lead Funk to argue that it "represents the ultimate
attempt to historicize the appearances of the risen Jesus by
making them physically palpable"?

22. What features of the story in John 21 of Jesus' appearance at
the seaside indicate that it is a later creation?

23. Why is it necessary to restore Peter? Why is this story in the
Fourth Gospel and not one of the synoptics? Are there hints
in other synoptic resurrection stories of Peter's restoration
after his betrayal of Jesus?

Unit IV

24. Make a list of those items that are common between the gospel of Peter and the canonical gospels. Do you see any pattern? This issue will be dealt with in detail in Arthur Dewey's essay later in this volume, but by paying close attention to the details of the text now you will be rewarded when you turn your attention to Dewey's argument.

25. The gospel of the Hebrews is an early Jewish Christian gospel that exists only in a few fragments quoted by others. It does not appear to be dependent on one of the synoptic Gospels although its sayings are synoptic-like. It is quoted in the early second century, so it most likely dates from the late first century. In this fragment the hero is James. Why would a Jewish–Christian community choose James as its resurrection hero? Remember that James is mentioned in Paul's list in 1 Cor 15, so why do you think James is missing from all the appearance traditions in the canonical Gospels?

26. Mark 16:9 is often referred to as the "longer ending" of Mark's Gospel. It only occurs in late manuscripts, not the earliest manuscripts of the gospel of Mark. What are the similarities between these stories and those in the gospel of Luke? Why would a scribe add such an ending to the gospel of Mark?

27. A number of scholars have argued that the Transfiguration stories in the synoptic Gospels were originally resurrection stories. What characteristics of the story suggest resurrection appearances to you? Why would Mark not have used this story as a resurrection story? What set of characteristics suggest it might not be a post-resurrection story?

28. If the miraculous catch of fish story in John 21 and Luke 5 are both derived from the same story, was it originally a resurrection story as in John 21 or a miracle story as in Luke 5? Do the parallels between these two stories convince you that they come from a common source? What would be your argument in each case?

29. Paul's list of appearances of the resurrected Jesus in 1 Cor 15 is the earliest reference to the resurrection we have. As we saw above he puts himself at the end of that list, but as

one who belongs on the list. These three narrations of Paul's experience from the book of Acts come from the end of the first century or the beginning of the second century. What does this late date about the narration indicate to you about when resurrection appearance stories began to appear in the tradition? What are the differences between Paul's description of this event in Galatians 1:13–17 and these stories in Acts?

30. The vision of Stephen in Acts 7 and the revelations to John of Patmos in the book of Revelations raise the question of the difference between resurrection appearances and visions. How would you describe these differences? Do you think they are real differences or imaginary ones?

31. You have now worked through all of the text in the New Testament and early Christian literature that we have about the resurrection. What would you say you have learned from this study? What do you see by putting the texts in chronological order? Do you see development? Elaboration? Trends? Contradictions?

Chapter 2
The Jesus Seminar Spring Meeting 1995

1. What is the difference between resurrection and resuscitation? Why is this distinction important?

2. To what evidence are the scholars pointing when they argue that the earliest experiences of the resurrection were visions of the resurrected Jesus or luminous apparitions?

3. Why would you think that the Romans would not turn the body of Jesus over to his friends?

4. In 1 Cor 15 where (in what geographical place) does Paul situate the appearances? What is the evidence for the original appearances of the resurrected Jesus occurring in Galilee? How strong do you think this evidence is? Why would the tradition preserve stories of appearances in both Galilee and Jerusalem?

5. If Paul is to be included in the list of those who saw the resurrected Jesus, then over what duration of time must those appearances have occurred? The Acts of the Apostles

picture the resurrection of the appearances as occurring over a period of 30 days, much too short a time period to include Paul. Why would the author of the Acts of the Apostles shorten the period to 30 days? Why would other Gospels want to lengthen the period?

6. Why would the seminar argue that the tradition developed from visions of the luminous figure to appearances of a more physical character?

7. Why is resurrection a matter of faith and not history?

8. Even though Mary of Magdala does not appear in Paul's list, the scholars appear inclined to think that she also had a vision of the resurrected Lord. What is the evidence for this? Why do you think they are making such an argument, while at the same time denying the appearances as reported in the Gospels of Luke and John?

Chapter 3

Robert M. Price, *Brand X Easters*

1. Price adduces a number of stories in which the body of the hero is not found and the assumption is that the hero is now among the gods. What light do these stories throw on the empty tomb stories in the Gospels? How strong do you think the parallels are between the stories Price adduces and the gospel accounts?

2. Some stories are meant to instruct the followers as to the meaning of the hero's life. Price uses the stories of Romulus and Appollonius for this purpose. Do you see any parallels to the gospel stories? Why might these stories have been told or created within the early communities?

3. The Asclepius story takes place in the dream, which is normal with stories associated with Asclepius. Are there dream stories in the Jesus tradition? Why is this type of story uncommon in the Jesus tradition?

4. In the case of the miraculous catch of fish, Price argues that the Pythagorean story is one from which the tradition of the fourth gospel is borrowing their version of the story. His evidence is the occurrence of the exact same number in both stories. How convincing do you find the argument and why do you find it convincing or unconvincing?

5. Price thinks the ascension of Moses as described by Josephus is so close to that of Luke that Luke must be dependent on the Josephus story. What are the parallels that you see between these two stories? How close are they? Do you agree with Price's assessment?

6. Price ends his essay with the question: "Were the Easter stories of the gospels typical of ancient Hellenistic myth and legend? You decide." So, what is your evaluation of the evidence Price has adduced?

Chapter 4

Arthur J. Dewey, *Resurrection Texts in the Gospel of Peter*

1. Funk in his collection of resurrection texts in the first essay of this volume had presented only the epiphany text from the Gospel of Peter. Dewey begins with both the death and epiphany text from the Gospel of Peter. Why does Dewey present both of these texts?

2. As you read this text, underline elements that you think are parallel to those in the canonical gospels. Do you see any pattern? Are there parallels to one gospel more than another? Does the Gospel of Peter know the canonical gospels and so is dependent upon them? Or are the synoptic gospels dependent upon the gospel of Peter? Or are they all dependent upon oral tradition? How would you settle this question? Can you settle this question? Must you settle this question?

3. Funk had placed the Gospel of Peter texts after the canonical gospels. Why did he do this?

4. What is the story of the suffering and vindication of the righteous one? Where does it come from?

5. What is the primary story of Dewey's reconstructed earliest layer of the Gospel of Peter? To what group of Jesus-followers would this appeal? What question(s) does it answer?

6. Dewey sees the earliest reference to God's vindication of Jesus in the phrase "he was lifted up." How does he use the story of the pattern of the suffering and vindication of the righteous one as the context in which to interpret this phrase? Do you find Dewey's argument convincing? If so, what does this say about how the earliest followers of Jesus came to terms with his death at the hands of the Romans?

Should this text be put as the first one in Funk's chronological list?

7. According to Dewey the details of "he was lifted up" are filled in by a later level of the Gospel of Peter with an epiphany story. This borrows from the language of apocalyptic. What are these apocalyptic details in the epiphany story?

8. Following Oziek, Dewey ties the empty tomb tradition to the mourning rites of women in the ancient world. Do you find this illuminates the women at the tomb in a new way? What effect do you think male attitudes towards women may have had in the preservation of the early traditions about the resurrection of Jesus?

Chapter 5
Roy W. Hoover, *Was Jesus' Resurrection an Historical Event?*

1. Hoover argues that the place to begin to understand what early Christians mean in their affirmation of Jesus' resurrection is what Judaism meant by resurrection. Why is this a sound methodological principle? What did Judaism mean by resurrection?

2. The earliest reference to resurrection in the Hebrew Bible (Christian Old Testament) is in the book of Daniel. What occasions the necessity for a belief in resurrection among Jews? How does the minority status of Jews within the Syrian empire and then the Roman empire effect belief in resurrection?

3. How does Jesus the martyr effect belief in his resurrection?

4. Hoover uses the mini-creed in 1 Cor 15:3–7 to argue that faith in Jesus' resurrection precedes chronologically the appearances of Jesus. What is the basis of his argument and do you find it convincing?

5. What is the significance for Hoover of Paul putting himself in the list of those who have seen the Lord?

6. The gospel resurrection stories are all different. Hoover argues that this indicates there is no common resurrection tradition. Why does he argue this?

7. What is the evidence that the empty tomb story was unknown to Paul? What is the evidence that it post-dates the writing of the Pauline letters?

8. In Hoover's translation of ancient resurrection faith into a
modern context, what does he argue is the essence of that
faith? How viable do you find that as an interpretation?

Chapter 6

Thomas Sheehan, *The Resurrection, an Obstacle to Faith?*

1. What does Sheehan mean when he says the Easter event is
not an historical event?

2. What for Sheehan is the significance of putting "resurrection" and "risen" in quotation marks? What is the difference between "resurrection" and resurrection? From what
or whom is he trying to distinguish his understanding of
"resurrection"?

3. On what evidence does Sheehan argue that exultation pre-
dates "resurrection" as an understanding of the Easter event?
Does this mean that the Philippians Hymn (Phil 2:6–11) and
the "he was lifted up" from the Gospel of Peter are the "earliest references of the "resurrection of Jesus"?

4. "To awake from sleep" is the literal meaning of the word
often translated "he was raised." What difference would it
make to your understanding of "resurrection" if you translated the phrase "he was awakened"? Sheehan terms this a
metaphor. Does this mean that "resurrection" is a metaphor?
If so, a metaphor for what?

5. "He was awakened" appears in the second stage. In what
New Testament text does the earliest reference to "he was
awakened" occur? Is there a story or narration of the events
of "resurrection" in the earliest level?

6. When Paul uses *egegertai* (he was awakened) or *ōphthē* (he
appeared) does he imply a physical activity? What does he
imply? What is Sheehan's evidence for his argument? Does
Paul know a narrative/story of the resurrection?

7. Only in the first gospel, Mark's, is there any story of the resurrection. What are the details of that story? Remember, the
gospel of Mark ends at 16:8. The other endings printed in
many Bibles are from a much later period.

8. How many years after the death of Jesus is it before narrative
images of the resurrection occur?

9. Why is the central methodological dividing line between a fundamentalist and critical approach to the resurrection, the dating of the texts, and their chronological arrangement?
10. What is the theological meaning of resurrection? How would you translate that into common, everyday experience?

Chapter 7
Thomas Sheehan, *How Did Easter Originally Happen? A Hypothesis*
1. Draw up your own image of the popular image of what happened at the resurrection.
2. Sheehan asks: "But if the gospel accounts of Easter are myths rather than historical accounts, what actually did happen after the crucifixion?" If the Easter accounts are myth, how can he ask such a question? What does he mean by myth? Historical account? What actually did happen?
3. As you read Sheehan's scenario what elements from the tradition is he drawing upon? Make a list.
4. As you draw up this list, how would you evaluate Sheehan's use of this material? How credible is his scenario? How would you modify it and why? How would you evaluate its historicity?
5. Arthur Dewey suggests in this volume that the rituals of women in mourning played a role in the emergence of the empty tomb story. Just as Sheehan has created an imaginative scenario for Peter, create such a scenario for Mary Magdala and the mourning rites of women.
6. Paul says in the 1 Cor 15:8 that Christ "appeared to him" and in Gal 1:16 God "was pleased to reveal his son to/in me." Three times the Acts of the Apostles (9:1–8; 22:6–11; 26:12–18) imagines this scene, although as Sheehan points out Paul's description is minimal, while Acts is quite elaborate. How would you compare the Paul tradition to the development of the Gospel resurrection stories? Is a similar pattern of development evident? From simple statement to elaborate story? Can you create an imaginative scenario for Paul? Where did the horse come from in the paintings of Paul's conversion?

Notes

Notes

Notes

Notes

Notes

CPSIA information can be obtained at www.ICGtesting.com
Printed in the USA
LVOW07s0013130916

504276LV00001B/79/P